"Chuck Bentley has done a masterful job in revealing the deceitfulness of riches and putting wealth in its right place. Fast reading with a deep understanding of what is really worthwhile. A great wake-up call to those climbing the wrong ladder."

Ken Eldred
AUTHOR, *THE INTEGRATED LIFE*

"In this book, Chuck Bentley moves beyond financial diet plan fads and points us in the direction of true abundant living. *The Root of Riches* lifts our gaze from simply cutting costs and clipping coupons to embracing God's vision of riches. A 'true north' book to orient the heart, not just the pocketbook!"

Rob Moll
EDITOR-AT-LARGE
CHRISTIANITY TODAY

"I admire Chuck Bentley and his efforts to help us think about our hearts and our treasure. God has said that if He cannot trust us with our finances, how could He trust us with real riches, i.e., the lives of men and women? I'm grateful for Chuck's leadership and testimony to help us trust God for true, eternal riches."

Steve Douglass
PRESIDENT
CAMPUS CRUSADE FOR CHRIST

"At a time when some are consumed with making money and others fearful of losing what they already have, Chuck wisely demonstrates how we can be rescued from such destructive worldly concerns, while prospering in an eternally significant manner. Readers will be challenged, enlightened and blessed!"

Rusty Leonard
FOUNDER AND CEO
STEWARDSHIP PARTNERS
INVESTMENT COUNSEL, INC.

"Chuck Bentley is the real deal. His book, *The Root of Riches,* takes readers straight to the heart of the matter: No one can be truly rich until he or she understands the three non-negotiables that he so clearly presents. This is a book for everyone, even those who think they know finances."

Hugh O. Maclellan
Executive Chairman
Maclellan Foundation, Inc.

"If, after 50 years of making films in Hollywood, I would be asked to recommend a group of individuals who not only know how to handle wealth, but understand the scriptural basis for accumulating it, Chuck Bentley would be at the top of the list. His new book, *The Root of Riches: What if Everything You Think about Money Is Wrong?* will be a life-changing revelation to young people, and a shocking change of direction for oldsters."

Dean Jones
Award-winning Actor

"Chuck Bentley has his finger on the pulse of the spiritual cancer ravaging the body of Christ. This book will give you insights into seldom identified but always present roots that lead to much grief. Chuck then presents clear directions to biblical solutions of money management."

Gunnar Johnson
Chairman of the Board
Christian Stewardship Network

"When it comes to thinking rightly about money, there are few people in this world that I respect more than Chuck Bentley. He is a man who walks his talk and, consequently, this book is a reflection of Chuck's personal belief system, which I have witnessed for many years. I respect Chuck and recommend this book to everyone who wants to think rightly about 'true riches.' This is a book to be read and to be given to those in our circles of influence who can stand a healthy dose of reality. This book puts money, riches and wealth in the proper (God's) perspective."

Ron Blue
AUTHOR, *MASTER YOUR MONEY*
PRESIDENT
KINGDOM ADVISORS

"If, like me, deep in your heart you are crying with the desire to acquire and leave a legacy of true wealth that will live on, you want to read and study this book. If you are a parent with children, a business person building a company, a missionary building a ministry or a pastor in a church, it should be a study guide for all of us.

"I plan to study its pages with my children and extended family and give it to many friends in different parts of the world. I know firsthand that this book is relevant whether you are in North, Central and South America, Europe, Africa, Asia or Oceania. It is a necessary and urgent work!"

Reginaldo Andre Kruklis
SENIOR PASTOR
INTERNATIONAL PROTESTANT
CHURCH, ZURICH, SWITZERLAND
FORMER PRESIDENT
HAGGAI INSTITUTE

"Chuck's new book is grounded in Scripture and frees us from our cultural assumptions on wealth and happiness. For the overworked, dissatisfied and weary, he offers a new definition of 'rich,' helping us to discover true wealth with conviction and clarity. Open *The Root of Riches* and be ready to have your ambitions redirected towards ultimate wealth and lasting satisfaction."

Peter Greer
PRESIDENT AND CEO
HOPE INTERNATIONAL
CO-AUTHOR, *THE POOR WILL BE GLAD*

"We live in the Age of Debt. Governments and individuals have lost their moorings. People grasp for behavior change, techniques and make rationalizations. I thank Chuck Bentley for courageously showing the connection between our roots and our fruit . . . how wrong treasures and gods have put our way of life and freedoms at risk.

"Truth shows us that every financial decision is a spiritual decision. May every reader dig deep, face truth and allow God to show them the life that is truly life!"

Jack Alexander

<small>Vice Chairman and Partner</small>
<small>Rainmaker Group</small>

"I have had the distinct privilege of watching Chuck's journey for many years and strongly encourage others to read this book! In this time of quick fixes, even in the realm of finances, debt and budgeting, Chuck will show the reader that true riches are found only in the person of Jesus Christ."

David Wills

<small>President</small>
<small>National Christian Foundation</small>

"In a time where it's easy to be anxious, fearful and focused on oneself regarding money, Chuck's new book debunks the myths and brings real truth which transforms, resulting in peace, hope and a generous life."

Daryl Heald

<small>Chairman</small>
<small>Giving Wisely</small>

THE ROOT OF
RICHES

WHAT IF EVERYTHING YOU THINK
ABOUT MONEY IS WRONG?

CHUCK BENTLEY

FORIAM
PUBLISHERS

Published by FORIAM Publishers in association with Crown Financial Ministries, Inc.

ISBN: 978-1-56427-285-0

Unless otherwise noted, verses are taken from The Holy Bible, New International Version®, NIV® Copyright © 1973, 1978, 1984, 2011 by Biblica, Inc.™ Used by permission. All rights reserved worldwide.

Verses identified as (NASB) are taken from the New American Standard Bible® (Updated edition), © 1960, 1962, 1968, 1971, 1072, 1973, 1975, 1995 by The Lockman Foundation. Used by permission.

Verses identified as (NKJV) are taken from the New King James Version. Copyright © 1982 by Thomas Nelson, Inc. Used by permission. All rights reserved.

Verses identified as (NLT) are taken from the Holy Bible, New Living Translation, copyright 1996, 2004. Used by permission of Tyndale House Publishers, Inc., Wheaton, Illinois 60189. All rights reserved.

Verses identified as (TLB) are taken from The Living Bible, © 1971 by Tyndale House Publishers, Inc., Wheaton, Illinois 60189. All rights reserved.

Verses identified as (ESV) are taken from The Holy Bible, English Standard Version, adapted from the Revised Standard Version of the Bible, copyright Division of Christian Education of the National Council of the Churches of Christ in the U.S.A. All rights reserved.

Verses identified as (AMP) are from the Amplified® Bible, © 1954, 1958, 1962, 1964, 1965, 1987 by The Lockman Foundation. Used by permission.

Verses identified as (KJV) are taken from the King James Version of the Bible.

Cover Design: Christopher Tobias
Interior Art and Layout Design: Josh Merriam, Sean Allen, Kevin Campbell
Editors: Jim Henry, Jim Armstrong

This book contains quotes from various individuals and references to a broad range of source materials. Any such mentions should not be viewed as an endorsement of the overall theological or political views of any particular person, nor (unless otherwise noted) as a recommendation of any particular book, article or website.

July 2011 Edition   Printed in the U.S.A.

CONTENTS

INTRODUCTION

Do not wear yourself out to get rich; do not
trust your own cleverness. Cast but a glance
at riches, and they are gone, for they will
surely sprout wings and fly off to the sky like
an eagle.[1]

As a child, our family fall ritual was for my parents to take my brother, two sisters and me to the Texas State Fair. Each year, I looked forward to the beautiful, crisp weather and a full day of experiences that dazzled the senses. In spite of the many forms of entertainment packed into the day: educational exhibits, the new car show, savory funnel cakes, foot long corny dogs, the farm animals petting zoo and souvenir shopping, I was always in a hurry to get to the Midway.

This was the wide avenue lined with carnival rides and games. Between the rides that produced fear or dizziness or both, were booths featuring games of skill and chance hawked by loud music, flashing lights, dangling prizes and the constant bellowing of carnival barkers.

"Step right up! Win a prize!" rang through the clatter of other competing noises.

Each game operator tried to entice me and throngs of others crammed into the Midway to buy a chance to win the "valuable prizes" hanging just inside the booths. They would lean out the tents and taunt the passing crowds by demonstrating how easy it was to knock down three milk bottles with a softball, toss a wooden ring over the top of a soda bottle or shoot a basketball through a hoop that looked close enough to touch. The chance to win a prize caused my adrenalin to rush and I was eager to prove my skills.

My usual modus operandi, or "M.O.," consisted of a brief surveillance of the area, holding on tight to my few allowance dollars as I tried to determine where the odds of winning were in my favor. Most of the booths were decorated with gigantic stuffed animals. Dogs, gorillas, snakes and sharks hung tantalizingly out of reach. Some of the grand prizes looked larger than me! After scouting the entire venue to sort through all the options, I would then select three or four places to take my chances. Sometimes my choice was determined by the prize; other times I pragmatically chose a game I thought I could win easily, regardless of the prize! I vacillated between the lure of winning a major prize and simply wanting to feel successful at something.

Every year, the results were the same. Whether I won a prize or not, I would always lose my money. Worse, I was enticed to lose even more! If I sunk only one of three basketballs into the hoop and two would have won, I was handed a plastic comb or a tiny stuffed animal that could then be "redeemed" for another try at the "grand prize." In other words, I either lost or got the sucker's prize to entice me into risking even more money for the BIG prize. What looked like a game of skill was more like gambling with the odds stacked in favor of the house.

Not surprisingly, my early adult years were spent walking through a real life Midway, seeking out and taking my chances with a variety of ways to get rich quick. Not only do I regret the vast number of mistakes I made in these failed attempts, but I regret even more the time that was spent so foolishly.

Like millions of others, I sought to blaze my own trail to riches. All the while, I fed on a steady stream of books, tapes and seminars that promised to make arrival at my desired destination a sure thing through self-help, increased motivation, "timeless" success principles and hot business opportunities. Today, those "opportunities" that once seemed so valid to me, I now see as only multibillion-dollar games of chance designed to separate people from their money. The "prize" is always the Holy Grail for the greedy: getting rich! They're games for suckers, and in those days, I was eager to play.

Look around. The world is still full of "carnival barkers" trying to lure in the get-rich-quick crowd on the Midway of life. They're just a little harder to spot. Instead of gaudy striped jackets and straw hats, they wear power suits and carry designer brief cases.

Like many, the desire to be rich had strong roots in my life. It grew beyond a mere financial goal; it became a status and an identity that I hungered to achieve. Although my relentless pursuit of it eventually drove me to the brink of financial ruin and beyond, I could not rest until it was mine. Something about getting rich and recognized as great caused my adrenalin to rush just like walking through the Midway so many years before.

In the pages ahead, I will share with you my own painful experiences trying to attain that elusive goal. You may recognize similar patterns in how you approach acquiring riches. More importantly, I will give you three non-negotiable truths that will put you on the path to growing really rich. My hope is that you learn from my mistakes and are spared the heartache, lost time and wasted energy that marked my journey and grow exceedingly rich on God's terms.

– Chuck Bentley

---

1. Proverbs 23:4-5

DEDICATION

I dedicate this book to the faithful steward, who knows that all the riches we have or may ever possess are found in Jesus Christ.

May you become a giant of a tree according to Isaiah's prophetic words:

> *They will be called oaks of righteousness, a planting of the Lord, for the display of His splendor* (Isaiah 61:3).

x

NON-NEGOTIABLE
NUMBER ONE

I ACCEPT THAT BOTH THE **CAUSE** AND
THE **SOLUTION** TO MY MONEY PROBLEMS
LIE WITHIN MY OWN HEART.

CHAPTER ONE: GETTING RICH

THERE IS NO CLASS SO PITIABLY WRETCHED AS THAT
WHICH POSSESSES MONEY AND NOTHING ELSE.
    – ANDREW CARNEGIE

Lena Mindy Rosenthal wanted to get rich. Born July 4, 1920 in Marbletown, New York to Polish immigrant parents, Lena dropped out of high school to seek her fortune at a variety of jobs before becoming a real estate broker.

By 1970, Lena—now "Leona"—was a wealthy chain-smoking workaholic on her third marriage. Her latest husband was multi-millionaire real estate investor Harry Helmsley. Helmsley had divorced his wife of 33 years to marry Leona on April 7, 1972. Together, they built an empire of plush New York City hotels and other successful real estate ventures. They became *billionaires*. Their wealth was backed by some of the most prestigious properties in the world: 230 Park Avenue, the Empire State Building and the Park Lane Hotel.

Harry Helmsley died in 1997, leaving Leona sole owner of their joint estate worth more than $5 billion. By most standards, Leona achieved her life's goal . . . she got rich, very rich.

Or did she?

By several accounts, Leona Helmsley had "zero" friends. She was even estranged from her only child, Jay Panzirer, a son from her first marriage. When Jay died of a heart attack at age 42, Leona sued her son's estate for money and property she claimed he had borrowed. At the time, her son's widow and her only four grandchildren lived in one of Leona's rental properties—but not for long. Leona's litigation wiped out the grieving family's finances, and when they couldn't pay the rent, she promptly evicted them.[1] No wonder she was called the "Queen of Mean."

Upon her death, Leona Helmsley left her dog, a Maltese named Trouble, a $12 million inheritance. It sounds like a bad pun, but Trouble had become Leona's only friend. Much of her estate, valued between $5 billion and $8 billion, went to a charitable trust to benefit *dogs*.[2] Trouble has since passed away, apparently intestate.

Would you say that Leona Helmsley was really rich? I suppose it depends on your definition of "rich."

Definitions of Being Wealthy

In their best-selling book, *The Millionaire Next Door*, Thomas Stanley and William Danko defined being wealthy this way:

> Ask the average American to define the term wealthy. Most would give the same definition found in Webster's. Wealthy to them refers to people who have an abundance of material possessions.
>
> We define wealthy differently. We do not define wealthy, affluent, or rich in terms of material possessions. Many people who display a high-consumption lifestyle have little or no investments, appreciable assets, income-producing assets, common stocks, bonds, private businesses, oil/gas rights, or timberland. Conversely, those people whom we define as being wealthy get much more pleasure from owning substantial amounts of appreciable assets than from displaying a high-consumption lifestyle.[3]

Notice anything unusual about their definition? These experts say that wealth is not a comparison of material possessions but actually a comparison of how many *appreciable* assets one owns. In their view, appreciable assets, or those that grow over time, are a better comparison of true wealth than material possessions. The difference is that appreciable assets *make* you money, while non-appreciable possessions *cost* you money for their purchase, upkeep and depreciation.

So, what about poor Leona? Well, since she owned an appreciable real estate empire worth billions, according to Stanley and Danko's *The Millionaire Next Door* definition, Leona Helmsley was indeed rich.

Want to Compare Yourself?

Did you know that America's poorest are far better off than the vast majority of the world's population? According to World Bank figures, the poorest 10% of Americans have more income than nearly four billion other inhabitants of planet Earth.[4]

So, how do you compare? Feeling any richer? My guess is that you're not. You've probably just discovered that you have more income than 90% of the world's population. Compared to the vast majority of individuals on earth, you're not just rich; you're fabulously wealthy. Shouldn't you be doing cartwheels?

...You're not just rich; you're fabulously wealthy.

If you're not overcome with joy, it could mean that something is seriously wrong with the world's definition of *rich.*

However, if you are willing to set that definition aside, you will learn what it means to be rich from God's perspective and a great new experience will open before you.

Rethinking Rich

Fidelity Investments, one of America's largest financial firms, recently surveyed 1,000 millionaires. Surprisingly, 42%

of them said they would need more than $7 million to feel truly rich.[5] Is this the new cultural definition of being rich?

Believe me, I can relate to the millionaires surveyed by Fidelity. I had my own number in mind of what I needed to acquire before I felt rich. My number was $10 million. It was not based on a financial plan or even logic, just a sense that I'd be a success in my own eyes once that goal was attained. The Fidelity survey left me wondering how many people actually consider themselves "rich."

In my research, I found a posting on a popular Web forum that sought an answer to this question:

Q: "How many rich people are there in the world?"

A: "It depends on how you define rich."

That was it . . . the only answer posted in the forum. It ended the conversation because that was the right answer! Interestingly, no one attempted to offer an alternative definition to what it means to be *rich*.

The amount and kind of wealth needed to feel rich covers a wide spectrum of standards. By Stanley and Danko's definition, we must accumulate a minimum of $1 million in assets that appreciate in value to consider ourselves rich. By Fidelity's research, Americans must achieve at least $7.5 million in assets to be rich. According to World Bank standards, you need only $20,000 of annual income to be *globally* rich.

I would submit to you that all of these definitions have one thing in common. They're all equally *unattainable.* No matter how much money or possessions you accumulate, you will never *feel* rich by this worldly definition.

There's a great scene in the old movie *Key Largo* that illustrates this point perfectly. Humphrey Bogart's character Frank McCloud and Lionel Barrymore's character James Temple are being held hostage by the gangster Johnny Rocco, played by Edward G. Robinson:

Rocco:	*There's only one Johnny Rocco.*
Temple:	*How do you account for it?*
McCloud:	*He knows what he wants. Don't you, Rocco?*
Rocco:	*Sure.*
Temple:	*What's that?*
McCloud:	*Tell him, Rocco.*
Rocco:	*Well, I want uh . . .*
McCloud:	*He wants more, don't you, Rocco?*
Rocco:	*Yeah. That's it. More. That's right! I want more!*
Temple:	*Will you ever get enough?*
McCloud:	*Will you, Rocco?*
Rocco:	*Well, I never have. No, I guess I won't.*[6]

The reason we'll never feel like we have enough is because none of the world's standards for being rich are biblical. They all fall short of reflecting an accurate view of what it means to be truly rich.

All of the world's standards for being rich are dominated by comparisons of what we can own or possess. Sadly, even the vast majority of Christians have not discovered that we can be rich with or without money, even though this principle is found throughout the Bible. In fact, God refutes the world's definition of rich in a single statement:

> *Then he said to them, "Watch out! Be on your guard against all kinds of greed; life does not consist in an abundance of possessions."*[7]

Mother Teresa, the Nobel Prize-winning nun who owned nothing, said: "Loneliness is the most terrible poverty." According to her, Leona Helmsley would be closer to a pauper than a tycoon because she suffered from the same deficit of love and companionship in her life as the abandoned street beggars and lepers of India.

Reaching the Ultimate Goal

In my pursuit of making the qualifiers list of the rich, I would never have reached for the Leona Helmsley billionaire status; that was over the top and seemed greedy. But the status of her pet, Trouble? Well, yes, but only if I could be the quiet, unassuming Millionaire Next Door type. I wanted $10 million but would live like I had less, a rationalization that made the goal of achieving worldly wealth more palatable.

Growing up, I saw so many episodes of the wildly popular TV series, *The Beverly Hillbillies,* that I can still repeat the theme song from memory:

> *Come and listen to a story about a man named Jed*
> *A poor mountaineer, barely kept his family fed,*
> *Then one day he was shootin' at some food,*
> *And up through the ground came a bubblin' crude.*
> *Oil that is, black gold, Texas tea.*
> *Well the first thing you know ol' Jed's a millionaire,*
> *Kinfolk said, "Jed move away from there!"*
> *Said, "Californy is the place you ought to be!"*
> *So they loaded up the truck and moved to Beverly . . .*
> *Hills, that is.*
> *Swimmin' pools, movie stars . . .*[8]

The plot was simple: Common man makes it big through no work or effort of his own! We could all relate to that dream come true.

My dream had only one variation: I didn't mind working hard to become rich and successful. After all, I had always been something of an overachiever in social, academic and athletic endeavors. I was Boy of the Week in grade school and voted Most Popular Student in Junior High. In high school I was accepted to the National Honor Society and voted Class Favorite and Student Body President, all while playing football, basketball, and running track. In college, I was Best Pledge, Pledge Class President, Outstanding Sophomore, Senior Man and Student Body President, again. You can see why I started to believe my own press clippings.

After graduating from Baylor University with a degree in business administration and being accepted to law school, I chose instead to begin a career in business. Quickly realizing that success in that field is widely measured by how much one makes, and sensing the need to prove myself, I became obsessed with acquiring wealth. No way would Chuck Bentley be a financial failure.

Like many others in corporate America, I knew of no other way to measure success than by net worth. For years, I considered myself the The Rich Young Wannabe. My bookcase was crammed with all the latest best-sellers on the topic of getting rich: *The Richest Man in Babylon*, *Think and Grow Rich* and *Rich Dad, Poor Dad*. Because I'd been a follower of Christ since the age of seven, my financial philosophy was a blend of self-help, pop culture and yes, biblical thought.

Still, I somehow had to reconcile my greed with being a Christian. I developed my own personal (and secret) definition of being rich:

Jesus + Lots of Money = Happiness.

What I wouldn't admit at the time, even to myself, was that the formula actually looked something like this:

Jesus   (a little of Him, but not too much)

+

Money   (as much as I could get without revealing my greed)

=   **The Perfect Balanced Portfolio.**

If you had accused me back then of loving money, not Christ, my defense would have been that this Perfect Balanced Portfolio was a great platform of influence and stature that God could use. Getting rich would be a validation of success, security and significance in the world's terms to help me influence others to seek success, security and significance on God's terms. A little confused, I know, but I considered my motives pure because I was willing (I thought) to "humbly" give God the credit. That was my story, and I was sticking with it.

Confident that one day my life would be a "rags to riches" triumph (forgetting that I was never in rags to begin with), my passion became the accumulation of money. Before long, unchecked greed led me to take foolish chances. My business endeavors and investments suffered more losses than gains. I saw these as temporary setbacks only and "doubled down" on even riskier ventures. Nothing could discourage me. The more I lost, the more intense became my drive to get rich. I was in full-blown denial.

They say the worst thing that can happen to one with a gambling mentality is to win. It's not surprising then that my quest to attain worldly riches continued uninterrupted for over 20 years, fueled by the occasional success. Sure, I'd taken my lumps, but I was still in the game and starting to catch up. Not rich yet, I wanted to believe I was getting closer and, for a while, it really looked that way.

While this private dream determined most of my behavior, an issue continually stood in my way to being completely controlled by it. I knew the Bible had something to say on this topic, and it seemed to contradict everything I was reading and everything I was attempting to accomplish. Pushing those concerns aside, another opportunity came along, and I reached for it with all of my heart and soul.

My Dot-com Dream

By the late 1990s, companies like Amazon and eBay were staking their claims in the mad rush to capitalize on the explosive growth of the World Wide Web with commercially viable uses or applications. The online business craze was similar to the 1849 California Gold Rush, and it captured my imagination as a ticket to the *Forbes'* list of rich and famous.

There had been many investment "bubbles" before the dot-com craze, including the "Tulip Bubble" of the 1630s and the "South Sea Bubble" of 1720. The problem with the dot-com bubble was that too many people had forgotten history's harsh lessons about investment bubbles, or if they remembered, they thought the old rules for caution no longer applied.

The investment mania that marked the late 1990s is described perfectly at Investopedia.com:

> *The dot-com bubble grew out of a combination of the presence of speculative or fad-based investing, the abundance of venture capital funding for startups and the failure of dot-coms to turn a profit. Investors poured money into internet startups during the 1990s in the hope that those companies would one day become profitable, and many investors and venture capitalists abandoned a cautious approach for fear of not being able to cash in on the growing use of the internet.*[9]

In an attempt to cash in on the dot-com fervor, my company was designed to serve as an online marketplace for business-to-business transactions. We would displace middlemen and brokers for Fortune 1000 companies.

My partners and I raised $1.2 million dollars in startup capital from a dozen highly qualified, sophisticated investors. Within months of our launch, we were recognized as one of the 60 best "Seed Stage" technology companies in the world. Looking back, much of it was hype, but then again, isn't that what drives irrational booms?

Riding the wave, we presented our business plan in a venture forum in Palo Alto, California and attracted even more potential investors, including an audience with Warburg Pincus, the famed equity investment firm in New York. Their offices, I would learn upon my visit, were located next to the even more famous (or infamous) Goldman Sachs.

By that time, my obsession had turned from finding new venture money to dreaming up ways to spend the millions of dollars I would earn when the company had its IPO (initial public offering).

With 175,000 shares of founder stock that I still held, plus many more performance-based options, my net worth looked spectacular. I was an Internet millionaire—on paper at least.

A bad IPO, or a pessimistic forecast, projected that our POP (public offering price) would open at $10 per share. With a great IPO, analysts projected that we might achieve a $100 per share price on opening day. If that were to happen, my plan was to purchase a professional sports franchise, unpretentiously, of course.

I will never forget Monday, March 13, 2000. That was the day I visited the offices of Warburg Pincus in New York City to pitch them my Internet dream company. The trip included a brief tour of the New York Stock Exchange. My stock would be traded on NASDAQ, but I was eager to understand the inner workings of Wall Street. While there, our guide explained, "Each day, the market opens with the ringing of the bell. Standing down there in the trading pits is like standing at the epicenter of the world."

It was a heady day for me, knowing my dreams were getting closer to becoming a reality. My imagination soared with the potential excitement of one day having my stock bought and sold by thousands of investors around the world.

Those elusive riches were now within reach.

DIGGING DEEPER

Chapter 1 – Getting Rich

Key Points

- The world has many definitions of "rich":

  - The World Bank's Global Rich survey – $20,000 annual income.

  - *The Millionaire Next Door* – A minimum of $1 million in appreciable assets.

  - Fidelity Investments Survey – $7 million to feel rich.

- It is easy to believe that more money is the answer to our problems.

Reflection

Read Luke 12:15.

1. How does Jesus' warning to the Pharisees apply to you today?

   guard against greed;
   life isn't defined by possessions

2. Mother Teresa said, "Loneliness is the most terrible poverty." What do *you* think is "the most terrible poverty"?

   not getting to be with the people
   I love

3. Have you ever thought that all you needed was just a little bit more?

4. In 20 words or less, what do you think it means to "be rich"?

5. What is the minimum amount of money you would need to have to think of yourself as being rich? (Be honest!)

6. Is there anything wrong with a person wanting to gain a profit from his or her business? Why or why not?

   As Christians, should we support businesses that give back to community vs. making the rich richer?

7. Chuck talks about how his "private dream" influenced much of his behavior. What do you think should be the primary influence in your life?

   God

8. What is Non-Negotiable No. 1?

Chapter 1 Endnotes

1. "Helmsley Grandkids Face Uphill Fight to Break Will," *New York Daily News*, Sept. 1, 2007. [http://www.nydailynews.com/gossip/2007/09/01/2007-09-01_helmsley_grandkids_face_uphill_fight_to_.html]

2. "Helmsley Left Dogs Billions in Her Will," *The New York Times*, July 2, 2008. [http://www.nytimes.com/2008/07/02/us/02gift.html]

3. *The Millionaire Next Door: The Surprising Secrets of America's Wealthy*, Thomas J. Stanley and William D. Danko, Taylor Trade Publishing, 1996

4. "True world income distribution, 1988 and 1993," Branco Milanovic, World Bank, 1999

5. Fidelity Investments [http://www.fidelity.com/inside-fidelity/individual-investing/millionaire-outlook-2011]

6. Imdb.com [http://www.imdb.com/title/tt0040506/quotes]

7. Luke 12:15

8. "The Ballad of Jed Clampett," Paul Henning

9. "Dotcom Bubble," Investopedia.com [http://www.investopedia.com/terms/d/dotcom-bubble.asp]

CHAPTER TWO: FROM RICHES TO
TRUE RICHES

AND IN ALL YOUR GETTING, GET UNDERSTANDING.

The apostle Paul's famous encounter with Jesus Christ came on the road to Damascus. While mistakenly believing he was accomplishing his religious duty, he was intercepted on the path that would have led to his own ruin. Instead of the Damascus Road, my encounter would come on Wall Street.

Ironically, on Monday, March 13, 2000, the very day I was in New York City to land an investor that would propel me to my dot-com dream, a chain reaction of bad news for technology stocks triggered a massive sell-off. Investors, fund managers and institutions began liquidating their tech positions. In just five days, the NASDAQ lost nearly nine percent, falling from 5,050 on March 10 to 4,580 on March 15. This is the day that history records the burst of the Internet bubble.

I remember naively hoping that my investors were not aware of all the bad news splashing in the headlines of *The Wall Street Journal*, *Barron's* and *Bloomberg*. My mind was racing for ways to keep the company and my personal ticket to the easy life alive. As if a spell had lifted, it seemed that everyone was suddenly aware that it was *crazy* to operate a company without positive cash flow or a realistic plan for achieving a profit. The winds of opportunity that had blown so promisingly at my back turned into a gale hitting me straight in the face. The venture was headed fast for rough waters.

The following week, a call with the Board of Directors revealed the obvious: They were well aware that the Internet boom was over. Worse, at the rate we were spending money, the company would run out of cash unless we found new investors and soon. As you would expect, they were nowhere to be found. We all acknowledged that the company had little chance of survival if the option to take the company public was closed.

After several weeks of analyzing every possible alternative, I recommended to the Board that the right decision was to cease operations, pay our staff and vendors and write off our losses. The dream was over.

Remember those 175,000 shares of stock I owned? Worthless. I would not be making my debut at the "epicenter of the world." No more Mr. Internet Millionaire, no more glowing, humble testimony of how God made it all possible. No more platform of influence and stature for God to use in His wisdom.

In an earlier stock market collapse, men leaped to their deaths from New York's tall office buildings. In a sense, when the dot-com bubble burst, I died too. Well, the "old" me died.

I certainly didn't realize it at the time. I was weeks away from becoming exceedingly wealthy by the world's standards. Then it was gone. In the days ahead, I began to realize that, like Paul, I'd had a "Damascus Road" experience. As with Paul, the seed of victory was hidden within my defeat. It had been planted some months before, so that when all appeared lost, a huge blessing was ready to burst through the surface and change my life.

Late in 1999, while I was working seven days a week, my wife, Ann, grew concerned about my irrational exuberance with the prospect of getting rich. She noticed I was consumed by the drive to take the company public. It was not just controlling all of my time, but my thoughts and energy, too. Ann noticed that my eyes "glazed over" unless the conversation was about the company.

Ann is the wise, quiet type, but when she starts talking, trust me, you want to listen. Her discernment had allowed her to see right through me, and she'd been watching the Perfect Balanced Portfolio become:

(Jesus) + **Internet Riches!** = My All-Consuming Passion in Life

Politely, Ann asked me to attend a Bible study at our church to learn "what the Bible says about money." I impolitely explained to her that I knew what the Bible said about money and if I needed to learn more about money I would take an adult education course in finance at the local community college which, oh by the way, was probably an excellent idea since we were going to have so much more money to manage when this brilliant company I was running went public in less than a year from its founding. Seriously, that's just how I talked at the time. Ugly, I know, but the truth is I was almost intoxicated with my pride.

By God's sovereign plan, however, Ann's prayers and persistence won over my stubborn will. I ended up in a Sunday night Bible study with four other couples and two singles to learn "what the Bible says about money." Mr. Internet Millionaire quietly and arrogantly sat in the room while others discussed all the Scripture that I already knew . . . or I thought I knew.

Looking back, I realize that before taking that study, I really only knew two verses about money: 1) Christians are not to love it, and 2) Christians are supposed to be generous. *Was there anything more to know?* Surely that knowledge would keep me from looking bad to the group. And besides, they would all soon enough be impressed with my business knowledge and the imminence of my becoming rich.

During the first week, it became apparent that I was not nearly as smart as I tried to act. The Bible is full of verses about money and possessions, and I had not read most of them in years; and even if I had, I viewed verses for what they could do for me and my pursuit of security, success and significance in the world.

What I was learning from the Bible began to loosen the tight grip that my wrong attitudes had on my heart. Verse after verse challenged all that I had believed about money, possessions and riches:

> So . . . if you have not been trustworthy in the handling of worldly wealth, who will trust you with true riches?[22]

What?!

Wait a minute . . . true riches? What am I missing? Have I been climbing the ladder to gain riches only to find out there is something bigger or better? Apparently, my ladder had been leaning against the wrong wall.

Was My Formula All Wrong?

I found within the Bible shocking insights that jarred my entire worldview.

Like a man staring in the mirror and seeing his distorted reflection, I was shocked by what I learned about myself. I was biblically illiterate for one. If that weren't humbling enough, I learned that *money* was my real Master. Although I worshiped God with my mouth, the Master that I *served* was not God. I came to realize that the Bible had a name for my attitude: Idolatry. Money was in fact the little god that controlled my life.

I found within the Bible shocking insights that jarred my entire worldview. I began to feel deep remorse for the way I'd been caught up in this Internet dream. My hidden formula for the Perfect Balanced Portfolio no longer added up. My identity as a man shaken, I kept quiet, not wanting to admit I was a fool.

A godly desire to hit the reset button began to grow. At 42, I wanted to switch direction in midstream and pursue what the Bible called true riches.

By week six of the 12-week study, hundreds of verses had pierced my heart and I was slowly changing from the inside. At the end of that week's session, the group facilitator asked the usual question, "Does anyone want to share what they got out of the lesson this week?" There was a long pause as I contemplated whether I should open my mouth or keep silent. What I had to say was not going to be easy for me to admit to a group of strangers.

My voice cracked before I could get out a single, coherent word. Tears filled my eyes. Ann was not yet aware of all that was going on in my heart, and she was surprised when I finally spoke in a near whisper, "Yes . . . I'd like to share what I've learned from the study."

The room immediately fell silent. The other participants eyed me curiously, no doubt wondering what the know-it-all was going to say. Ann, ever the supportive wife, simply patted my arm to encourage me.

"When I began this study, I thought I knew everything about money. I really didn't want to be here, and I thought this was a huge waste of my time."

That didn't seem to catch anybody by surprise. I struggled on, but if you've ever tried to publicly express a deep sense of remorse, you know how difficult it was to continue. I was choking back tears.

"What I have learned is that I am an *idolater.*" Now I really had their attention.

"Money has been my idol for years. In these past several weeks, I've recognized that this is a sin equal to any other act of immorality. I repent of my sin, and I want to serve God, not money. I want the *true* riches that God promises those who are faithful to Him."

Indescribable Peace

Little did I know how much my life would change from
that day forward. It was only a matter of months until the dot-
com bubble burst, taking my dream of worldly riches with it.
What I didn't realize at the time was that God was preparing
me for what lay ahead. So when the bottom fell out, instead of
wanting to take an elevator to the top floor to end it all, I actually felt peace. I had been set free.

Thomas Aquinas said, *"The highest manifestation of life consists in this: that a being governs its own actions. A thing which is
always subject to the direction of another is somewhat of a dead
thing."*[3]

The thirteenth-century theologian rightly declared that life
in its fullest, most meaningful sense is a life of *freedom.* The very
thing I thought was my ticket to freedom was actually holding
me prisoner. By studying and applying what God's Word says
about money, I escaped the invisible "master" that had dictated
my actions for well over 20 years.

God set me free from the pursuit of worldly wealth to seek
riches on His terms. To be a Christian means believing in, trusting and accepting Christ as Savior. Every Christian does this.
It's the next step, however, where so many of us falter: serving
Christ as *Lord.* I now wanted to take that step. I wanted God to
take His rightful seat on the throne of my heart.

I sought the meaning of *true* riches with the same passion
and dedication with which I once pursued worldly wealth. I
poured over God's Word for the first time since becoming an
adult. Although I'd grown up in a Christian home and many
verses were familiar to me, I had never been a serious student of
the Bible nor had I applied its teachings to my life. Day after day,
I rose before dawn and prayed, "Lord, I am here to read Your
Word so that I may meet with You. Please help me to know You
more so that I may love You more in order to serve You more."

God has been faithful at every turn to answer that prayer.
In my quest, I've come to understand the root of true, eternal

riches from a biblical perspective, and I'll share with you some wonderful discoveries in the chapters ahead.

God's Word is clear that you, too, can be rich—with or without money—if you are willing to make certain changes in your heart and mind. Human beings were designed to worship. You can't help it. If you won't worship God, you will worship something else, whether it's your job, your kids, your money, or even yourself.

You might give lip service to the notion of subjecting yourself to God's control, but don't be deceived; we are all controlled by what we love. If you love God, His control is an easy yoke to bear. If you love money, it will become an intolerable burden on your life. To change the way you relate to money and possessions, you must change your innermost affections. Your heart must be changed before you can be truly rich.

To make this life-altering change, we must start by examining our *roots*.

Roots, Trees and You

Think of a Bible verse about money—just anything that pops into your head. Odds are pretty good you landed on *"For the love of money is the root of all evil."*[4]

1 Timothy 6:10 may be the best known but least understood Bible verse by Christians and non-Christians alike. A lot of people can quote it, but few really know what it means.

Recently, on a plane traveling to Colorado, I sat next to a couple in the bulkhead row. We had a very brief exchange when they asked me what I do for a living.

I gave them a straight but gentle answer. "Well, I teach people what the Bible says about money."

Without hesitation, the husband offered his thoughts, "I know what it says. I know exactly what the Bible says about money." He paused as if to think briefly, "Money is the root of all evil."

As he waited for my reply, there was an awkward moment because the look on his face indicated he was confident that he had properly answered a tricky trivia question. He seemed pretty proud of himself, even though his answer was wrong.

Of course, that's like a hanging curveball for anyone who's spent more than a few hours studying Bible verses about money. It's easy to hit that one out of the park.

"Well, not exactly," I said with more than a hint of smugness as I corrected the man. "There's another word in there. The verse you are thinking of actually says the *love* of money is the root of all evil."

My fellow passenger gave the required "ah," feigning he was impressed with my profound biblical acumen, yet I couldn't escape the nagging feeling that I, too, had missed something in the often-misquoted verse.

After the flight, I decided to revisit 1 Timothy 6:10. As I studied the verse, I sensed the Holy Spirit leading me to a deeper understanding. I looked at each word and meditated on the major elements: love . . . money . . . evil. What was I missing? Then, as if the Holy Spirit were speaking right to me, I heard, "You're missing a key word here. Look closer at the word *root*."

I had missed it the whole time. Why is it there? Why is the love of money, an evil that Christians are to avoid, described as *a root*?

Let's put the verse in context. First, it was given as a warning from the apostle Paul to Timothy. Paul knew that his young protégé would one day carry on his work of advancing the first century church. The apostle wanted to protect the Church and enable it to grow.

Digging deeper, we see that the love of money is a sin we internalize, taking it deep into the heart. It requires a suitable analogy to give it meaning. That meaning was vital not only to Timothy 2,000 years ago; it's just as important for you and me today.

Dwelling on that meaning caused me to think of the roots of a tree. Lots of things have roots, but they always make me think of trees. Trees have roots—big ones.

Then there was that voice again. "How many trees are mentioned in the Bible?"

Almost as a lark, I decided to check. You know what I found? There are far more trees mentioned in the Bible than I ever imagined.

I found pomegranate, mustard, balsam, olive, tamarisk, poplar, fig, nut, incense, sycamore, pine, apple, cedar, oak, broom, myrtle, almond, and palm trees mentioned throughout God's Word.

The Bible often uses the image of a tree to illustrate a truth, sometimes describing a given tree as good or bad.

Perhaps the best known example of this occurs in Genesis, when the Lord plants two trees in the Garden of Eden. We see the tree of life, a good tree, and the tree of knowledge of good and evil, a decidedly *bad* tree that Adam and Eve were warned to avoid at all costs. The very beginning of mankind's existence is related to the choice between two trees.

Of all of the trees mentioned in the Bible, including those revealed in the Garden, I believe those most crucial for us to understand today are the trees used to describe us, you and me.

I'll leave it to you to ponder whether you're a good tree or a bad tree. Just understand that Scripture compares us to trees. We are to become like trees that bear good fruit.

> *"No good tree bears bad fruit, nor does a bad tree bear good fruit. Each tree is recognized by its own fruit. People do not pick figs from thorn bushes or grapes from briars. The good man brings good things out of the good stored up in his heart. And the evil man brings evil things out of the evil stored up in his heart."*[5]

Let's call this evil tree, as described by Jesus, the "Me Tree." It represents a person born into this world in a natural state (what the Bible defines as a fallen state) without the Spirit of God living in him or her. This tree sees the world as something we can own and possess. It looks at acquiring riches through possessions.

Then we have the good tree, a person who has the Spirit of God living in him or her. Let's call that person the "He Tree," representing that He, God, lives within. The term has nothing to do with human gender. There are male and female He Trees.

When we ask Christ to come into our hearts as Lord, we become His possession, a He Tree. This tree understands that God owns everything. It looks at riches from God's perspective, knowing that it is a steward and not an owner. The tree and everything on it comes from and belongs to the Lord. Psalm 24:1 makes this clear, *"The earth is the Lord's, and everything in it, the world, and all who live in it."*

If we are trees and expected to bear good fruit, it's important to understand the root system, because it's crucial to our ability to bear good fruit.

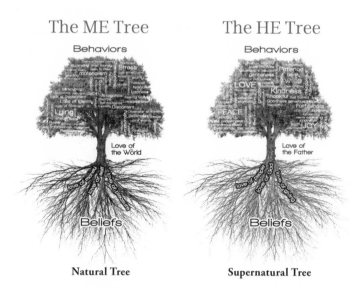

In the next chapter, we'll dig down to get a closer look at the roots of our Me Trees and He Trees.

DIGGING DEEPER

Chapter 2 – From Riches to True Riches

Key Points

- The world has a well-defined system of acquiring riches but God has His own system by which we can acquire true riches.
- We are considered to be like trees in the Bible.
- The love of money is a root cause of many evils.

Reflection

6:6 msg

- Read 1 Timothy 6:10. Ask God to speak to your heart and give you fresh insight into the depth of this passage.

- Read Luke 6:43-45 and consider the importance of what is stored up in our hearts. *What's in ♡ comes out of me*

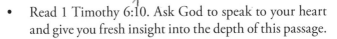

- Thomas Aquinas said, *"The highest manifestation of life consists in this: that a being governs its own actions. A thing which is always subject to the direction of another is somewhat of a dead thing."*

1. Have you subjected your life to the control of money and possessions, or are you controlled by God alone?

2. What do you need to do if you are a captive to financial bondage?

3. Chuck says, "The seed of victory was hidden within my defeat." What does he mean?

4. Write out what would be your Perfect Balanced Portfolio.

    _____ + _____ =

    _____

5. Chuck believes that the Bible is a relevant guide for money issues. Do you agree? Why or why not?

6. How does a tree's root system affect the quality of fruit it produces?

7. What do you really love? Are you controlled by it? If so, how?

    people   sometimes

8. Write Non-Negotiable No. 1 for getting truly rich in the space below.

Chapter 2 Endnotes

1. Proverbs 4:7 (NKJV)

2. Luke 16:11

3. http://www.brainyquote.com/quotes/
    authors/t/thomas_aquinas_3.html

4. 1 Timothy 6:10 (KJV)

5. Luke 6:43-45

CHAPTER THREE: GETTING INTO OUR ROOTS

What better way to understand trees and roots than to start with a seed?

Did you know that pine cones contain seeds? At home I have a tiny cone, less than two inches long. It's packed with very small seeds. I keep it as a reminder that many of us feel small and insignificant, unaware that God can use the smallest of seeds for significant purposes.

Seeds are dynamic. It may look like nothing is happening inside, but when one falls to ground, its internal machinery starts cranking; it germinates and begins to grow.

The seed first sends out tiny roots that form the beginning anchor that will hold it in the ground. Without that firm foundation, our seed could never become a tree. God designed it that way. Do you see the irony in something having to be buried in the ground in order to come to life? In John 12:24, Jesus refers to a grain of wheat *dying* before it can produce a new harvest.

We must be willing to die to ourselves before we can become rooted in Him.

Characteristics of Roots

There are three primary characteristics of roots.

First of all, they're *not visible.* In most cases, a root is beneath the surface of the ground. For the most part, you can't see the roots of a tree.

Secondly, roots are *pervasive.* Did you know that the root systems of most trees resemble in size and complexity their trunks and branches above ground? In fact, some trees have a radius of roots 4 times larger than their crowns. Roots can spread out, *way out,* in search of food and water.

Finally, roots are *responsible for the fruit* of the tree. If a tree has good roots, it will usually produce good fruit. Conversely, bad roots, bad fruit.

My Hands-on Experience

I had my own experience with roots recently when a tree died in my backyard. Note to tree huggers: I did *not* kill it for purposes of this illustration. I'm not sure why it died, but I promised Ann I would dig it up and remove it from our yard, stump and all.

Here's a drawing of the offending stump. The band on the trunk indicates ground level before I started digging. The stump looked pretty small and I could wiggle it back and forth. Like most men, I thought I could just dig a little

BELOW GROUND

and then yank the thing up and be done with it. Sadly for my back, that would not be the case.

I started digging a little hole around the base of the stump, trying to loosen it up, or at least get an idea of where the roots ended. That wasn't happening, so I kept digging and the hole kept expanding. Before long, I had a great big hole.

I kept digging to find the end of the roots. There was no end of the roots! What I thought would be a quick chore turned into hours of backbreaking work. I lost track of time, but at some point, our two youngest boys, John and Luke, joined the fight. We dug, sawed, chopped and even tried pulling out the stump with a rope.

Finally, after a half day of hard labor, the stump gave way and came out of the ground. It held one more surprise for me, unfortunately. With all that digging, I'd failed to notice that mixed in with the tree's roots were roots from another species entirely—poison ivy! It was a gift that kept on giving.

> *The love of money is like a root....*

After all that effort to remove this seemingly small tree stump, it gave me a clear visual of why Paul used a root to describe a very stubborn and pervasive problem: *The love of money is like a root. . . .*

It's a serious issue. Getting rid of bad roots is not an easy proposition, but it has to be done if you want to bear good fruit.

Scripture also uses the image of trees to describe you and me. As trees, we have roots. The problem is, we're born into this world with *flawed* roots that are pervasive, growing hidden beneath the surface and controlling our lives.

Born a Me Tree

All trees have primary and secondary roots. The primary roots of a Me Tree, that's the one without the Spirit of God, are the love of self, the love of money, and the love of pleasure.

Notice the interrelationship of love that unites money, self and pleasure. These form the identity of the tree.

love of money
love of self
love of pleasure

This is an illustration of the essence of the world's "root system." It's what makes the world go 'round. We are born with this root system and it's the reason we are all alienated from God. Like Adam, we lost our high position with the fall. "In Adam's fall, we sinned all."[1]

We keep the primary roots of our Me Tree hidden for obvious reasons. No one wants to wear a sign saying, "I love myself, I love money, and I love pleasure." We won't admit it, so we hide it. But these roots are not hidden from the Lord.

Very early in the Bible, the Lord warned the Israelites about these roots:

> There may come a day when you say to yourself, "My power and the strength of my hands have produced this wealth for me."[2]

Notice how the Bible words this warning? They will boast to themselves! The Lord revealed to them that they would not openly express their attitude towards money and riches, but would keep it to themselves. The Israelites, like you and me, were denying the truth that everything they owned had actually come from God as a demonstration of His kindness.

"This wealth is mine. I earned it. I deserve it. I'm going to keep it for myself." This attitude persists even today when we are deceived by the world's lie that convinces us we are responsible for our own success.

Preceding this warning the Lord gave the Israelites a clear picture of how this root grows and develops:

> *When you have eaten and are satisfied, praise the Lord your God for the good land he has given you. Be careful that you do not forget the Lord your God, failing to observe his commands, his laws and his decrees that I am giving you this day.*
>
> *Otherwise, when you eat and are satisfied, when you build fine houses and settle down, and when your herds and flocks grow large and your silver and gold increase and all you have is multiplied, then your heart will become proud and you will forget the Lord your God, who brought you out of Egypt, out of the land of slavery. He led you through the vast and dreadful wilderness, that thirsty and waterless land, with its venomous snakes and scorpions. He brought you water out of hard rock. He gave you manna to eat in the wilderness, something your ancestors had never known, to humble and test you so that in the end it might go well with you.*[3]

The central issue of all problems created by and with money is a proud heart.

Feeder Roots

The Me Tree also has a secondary root system comprised of *feeder roots*. These roots branch out in search of food and water to feed the growth of the tree.

Like the stubborn roots of that tree my boys and I pulled out of the backyard, the Me Tree's feeder roots flourish in the soil of this world and become very, very pervasive.

The Trouble with Books

Mark Twain, the great American author and humorist stated, "I am opposed to millionaires, but it would be dangerous to offer me the position."[4]

Almost as pervasive as the feeder roots of the Me Tree are books about making mountains of money. Publicists seeking endorsements or promotional support for their authors have sent me quite a few of them, and most should be in the fiction section. It's safe to say that, usually, only the authors and publishers are cashing in.

The underlying premise for these books is always the same: *More money means a better life.* It's such an easy sell because most people actually believe it—as much as they believe in the law of gravity. They just won't admit it. Before my dot-com debacle, I devoured these tomes of "wisdom," hoping to find the one mysterious nugget that would make me rich. Now, they rarely get a second glance.

Still, one book recently caught my eye. It was *The Five Lessons a Millionaire Taught Me about Life and Wealth* by bestselling author Richard Paul Evans. Well, it was really the dust jacket that got my attention. It claimed the book was, "ONE OF THE MOST POWERFUL BOOKS EVER WRITTEN ABOUT MONEY."

I have no idea how many books have been written about money, but I'd guess it's in the tens of thousands, if not more. So while these books usually go in the "round file," this one's claim was so provocative, so "IN YOUR FACE," that I decided to flip through the pages to see what the author believed about money and riches.

The story begins with an anonymous millionaire talking to the author's church youth group. The author is only twelve years old at the time, and living in a home experiencing great financial hardships.

The anonymous millionaire pulls a $100 bill from his wallet and holds it up. Evans could only stare in wonder. He had never seen one before.

The anonymous millionaire then asks, "Is money evil?"[5]

Another enthralled teenager offers, "The Bible says that money is the root of all evil."

Apparently prepared for this answer, the anonymous millionaire pounces.

"You are referring to . . . 1 Timothy, Chapter 6, Verse 10 . . . and it does not say that. It says that the love of money is the root of all evil. There's a big difference. In fact, just one chapter earlier in Timothy, the apostle Paul says if 'any provide not for his own, he hath denied the faith, and is worse than an infidel.' How can you provide for your own without money?"

This, of course, is entirely accurate, and a great illustration of how 1 Timothy 6:10 is almost universally misquoted. Recall the earlier conversation with my fellow airline passenger. The real nugget here, however, is that while the verse does not condemn money, neither does it give us a blank check to pursue it with reckless abandon.

Evans is enlightened by the anonymous millionaire's special knowledge and no longer forced to wallow in his family's financial hardships. He is free to pursue riches.

God is not promising earthly riches, but His abundant blessing.

Bad enough, but the author goes on to claim that the Bible offers us "financial *karma*" (emphasis mine), a decidedly unbiblical concept. Even more disturbing is his interpretation of Malachi 3:10:

> *"Bring the whole tithe into the storehouse, that there may be food in my house. Test me in this," says the Lord Almighty, "and see if I will not throw open the floodgates of heaven and pour out so much blessing that you will not have room enough for it."*

Evans' take is that generosity "feeds the soul, and ironically, it also feeds the pocketbook."[6]

This is the "prosperity gospel," or the give to get philosophy. In the verse, God is not promising earthly riches, but His abundant *blessing*. There's a difference and it may or may not have anything to do with your pocketbook. If you truly felt the

Lord's blessing in your life, trust me, you'd be a lot less concerned about what is in your wallet.

Mr. Evans gives a lot of money to charity and he's probably a very nice man, but the prosperity gospel, give money to get money, is wrong, fruitless and even dangerous. What happens when someone follows it and then is not rewarded with earthly riches? Will he not feel betrayed and turn away from God? Love, gratitude and obedience should motivate our giving, not the expectation of money in return.

Finally, in my view, the Bible stands alone as the most powerful book ever written about money. It is important that you know what it actually says, so you are able to rightly discern the validity of all other philosophies and opinions on money, possessions and wealth.

How to Spot a Me Tree

It is not wrong to have an abundance of money and possessions. However, it is wrong to be a Me Tree. The Me Tree is alluded to throughout the Bible, because the Lord knows exactly how this tree operates. Once its primary roots—the love of self, money and pleasure—have taken hold in the heart, the secondary roots go in search of food to keep the tree growing and to satisfy its desires. Our fallen world is filled with all the food the Me Tree is so desperately seeking.

These characteristics will help you identify the Me Trees around you. These are people with their root systems firmly entangled in the world.

- **They run after things.**

Things are very important to the Me Tree. In fact, they run after them.

> So do not worry, saying, "What shall we eat?" or "What shall we drink?" or "What shall we wear?" For the pagans run after all these things, and your heavenly Father knows that you need them.[7]

- **They are greedy for money**.

Me Trees will do practically anything to get ahead. According to the apostle Peter, even people in the church, doing "the Lord's work" can use their positions for personal gain.

> Be shepherds of God's flock that is under your care, watching over them—not because you must, but because you are willing, as God wants you to be; not pursuing dishonest gain, but eager to serve.[8]

- **They are eager to get rich**.

Me Trees are preoccupied with opportunities to make excessive amounts of money. Relationships with others are carefully calculated for their economic value.

> Those who want to get rich fall into temptation and a trap and into many foolish and harmful desires that plunge people into ruin and destruction.[9]

- **They think godliness is a means to financial gain**.

Some of the best examples of Me Trees teach the prosperity gospel, attempting to convince *others* that godliness is a means to financial gain. Ever notice how they really seem to enjoy money *themselves*? It's no coincidence. Their personal doctrine is a feeder root tapped right into the love of money, but they use the Bible to justify it. The Lord calls these false teachers out and warns us to run from their teaching.

> If anyone teaches otherwise and does not agree to the sound instruction of our Lord Jesus Christ and to godly teaching, they are conceited and understand nothing. They have an unhealthy interest in controversies and quarrels about words that result in envy, strife, malicious talk, evil suspicions and constant friction between people of corrupt mind, who have been robbed of the truth and who think that godliness is a means to financial gain.[10]

- **They live with the desire to eat, drink and be merry.**

Me Trees seek to satisfy their every desire and view the increase of comfort and pleasure as the ultimate reason for living. They crave only to be comfortable and happy. Pleasure is their purpose.

> *And I'll say to myself, "You have plenty of grain laid up for many years. Take life easy; eat, drink and be merry."* [11]

- **They have a continual craving for more money.**

Me Trees love money and can't get enough of it. Their feeder roots restlessly seek out more and more and are never satisfied, no matter how much wealth they acquire.

> *Whoever loves money never has enough; whoever loves wealth is never satisfied with their income. . . .* [12]

- **They are deceived by wealth and the desire for more things.**

Some Me Trees are fully aware of what the Bible says about obedience, generosity and loving our neighbors. Their feeder roots, however, have choked off the Word of God and killed the good fruit.

> *Still others, like seed sown among thorns, hear the word; but the worries of this life, the deceitfulness of wealth and the desires for other things come in and choke the word, making it unfruitful.* [13]

- **They place their hope and security in wealth.**

This is the most common trap for the Me Tree. It stores its hope and trust in his bank account instead of in God. Since he is always vulnerable to life's uncertainties, he cannot have real peace and, therefore, never any spiritual growth.

> *Command those who are rich in this present world not to be arrogant nor to put their hope in wealth, which is so uncertain, but to put their hope in God, who richly provides us with everything for our enjoyment.*[14]

• **They lose all contentment**.

This Me Tree is never happy and always needs more security, success and significance.

> *Keep your lives free from the love of money and be content with what you have, because God has said, "Never will I leave you; never will I forsake you."*[15]

• **They covet other people's things**.

One of the most ignored of the Ten Commandments is not to covet your neighbor's things. A Me Tree is always comparing its lot in life with others and wanting what they have acquired. It cannot be happy for the success of others.

> *You shall not covet your neighbor's house. You shall not covet your neighbor's wife, or his male or female servant, his ox or donkey, or anything that belongs to your neighbor.*[16]

• **They will sneer at Jesus' teaching and ultimately reject His Words**.

Me Trees can be very "religious," but their feeder roots have no discernment for the truth. Jesus' teachings hold no special meaning. These Me Trees are indiscriminate and they'll feed on the nuttiest ideas to satisfy their unmet lust for wealth or fame. By the way, the world is all too happy to supply those crazy philosophies. Remember the "carnival barkers" dressed in business suits?

> *The Pharisees, who loved money, heard all this and were sneering at Jesus.*[17]

A Million Dollars in Hopes

On November 15, 1903, Charles Ponzi stepped off the *SS Vancouver* onto the docks of Boston, an immigrant from Italy with a dream of becoming wealthy in America.

Like many immi-
grants, Ponzi worked
several jobs and tried
many different business
ventures in the years
ahead, all with the aim
of achieving success in
his new home. Unlike
most immigrants, he
was not averse to cross-
ing the line between
legal and illegal. By
1919, he'd had several

*Ponzi aka "Charles Bianchi"
under arrest circa 1910*

scrapes with the law, mostly for fraud, and had served time in prison.[18]

None of that would keep Ponzi from his quest to be rich, however. In that year, he began implementing the infamous scheme that today bears his name.

Charles Ponzi was certainly not the first to rob his fellow man by promising absurdly high returns on investments; no doubt he learned from others who had tried it before him. In general, a "Ponzi Scheme" works by giving older investors high returns drawn from money taken in by new investors. The money isn't really invested in anything, just passed around. The first people in appear to make a lot of money. That's what really gets the scheme snowballing.

The scheme is spread by word of mouth, drawing in more and more money from new investors with dollar signs in their eyes. As long as enough money is coming in, the scheme goes on. At a certain point, however, more money is needed to pay the old investors than is coming in from the new, and the entire house of cards collapses.[19] By the time Ponzi's scheme collapsed, he reportedly was raking in $1 million a week. In all, investors lost between $7 million and $15 million.[20]

Needless to say, when the law caught up with him, Ponzi went back to prison. If ever there was a Me Tree, it was Charles Ponzi. He would later tell *The New York Times*, "I landed in this country with $2.50 in cash and $1 million in hopes, and those hopes never left me."[21]

You would think that we would have learned from this tragic story of deception and loss brought about by a man filled with "$1 million in hopes" (translation: $1 million of greed). But instead, Ponzi's story has been repeated many times over around the world. It is an example of the truth of God's Word: "What has been will be again, what has been done will be done again; there is nothing new under the sun."[22]

Affinity Fraud

In 2009, Bernie Madoff was convicted of a "Ponzi scheme" that lasted for more than twenty years with estimated losses for investors in excess of $21 billion. His fraud is far and away the largest in the world. The size, scope and duration of Bernie Madoff's con made Ponzi look like the amateur he was.

Bernie Madoff

Madoff's sophisticated scam fooled some of the brightest minds in the world. In the same year, Tom Petters, a Minnesota businessman, was convicted of a "Ponzi scheme" estimated at more than $3.65 billion. It lasted more than a decade, earning him infamy for pulling off the second largest con in history.

Tom Petters

Appropriately, Madoff received a sentence of 150 years in federal prison; Petters, received 50 years.

These two recent examples of massive fraud share many common traits with the original scheme of Charles Ponzi, with one notable difference. Madoff is Jewish and Petters is a "professing" Christian. Each used his status within those respective social groups to con victims into thinking their investments were safe. After all, "He's one of us, right?" This is called affinity fraud, because the con man takes advantage of the victim's natural liking or comfort level with him. It's a huge betrayal, and I think a perfect illustration of how low a Me Tree will go in the pursuit of earthly riches.

The Question Begging to Be Answered

The Jewish community understandably feels betrayed by Bernie Madoff. Untold news stories and blogs carried comments by Jewish religious leaders expressing shame and outrage at his behavior.

Many of these observers shared a sense of bewilderment that one of their own could do this. Rabbi David Wolpe of Sinai Temple in Los Angeles told *The New York Times*, "Jews have these familial ties. It's not solely a shared belief; it's a sense of close communal bonds, and in the same way that your family can embarrass you as no one else can, when a Jew does this, Jews feel ashamed by proxy. I'd like to believe someone raised in our community, imbued with Jewish values, would be better than this."[23]

The habitat of the Me Tree is worldwide, so we shouldn't be surprised when one finds fertile ground around us. The question begging to be answered is, "What was missing in Bernie Madoff and Tom Petters that allowed them to sleep at night while they stole the life's savings of so many people?"

As we shall see, the Bible gives a simple, but profound answer.

DIGGING DEEPER

Chapter 3 – Getting into Our Roots

Key Points

- Our natural roots have three primary characteristics.

- We are all born into the world as Me Trees.

- Me Trees have clear beliefs that control their behaviors.

- Bernie Madoff and Tom Petters scammed others in their own community in spite of their outward religious behavior.

Reflection

1. Read Deuteronomy 8:6-10. What is the "test" the Lord is administering to His people?

   remembering Him, keeping commandments in the rich life He provides

2. Read Ecclesiastes 5:10. What is the connection between the heart and money in this passage?

   $ doesn't fulfill/ provide contentment

3. How would you answer the question: "What was missing in Bernie Madoff and Tom Petters that allowed them to sleep at night while they stole the life's savings of so many people?"

4. Try to repeat from memory Non-Negotiable No. 1.

    How can you apply this truth to your current financial circumstances?

5. What are the three primary roots of the Me Tree?

6. What are some basic characteristics of a Me Tree's "feeder roots"?

7. Would your spouse or your friends classify you as a Me Tree? Would their assessment be correct? Why or Why not?

8. What makes "affinity fraud" so insidious?

Chapter 3 Endnotes

1. *New England Primer*, believed to be the first textbook printed in the American Colonies

2. Deuteronomy 8:17

3. Deuteronomy 8:10-16

4. Mark Twain

5. *The Five Lessons a Millionaire Taught Me about Life and Wealth*, Richard Paul Evans. Aurcadia Press, 2004, pg. 4

6. Ibid., pg. 92

7. Matthew 6:31-32

8. 1 Peter 5:2

9. 1 Timothy 6:9

10. 1 Timothy 6:3-5

11. Luke 12:19

12. Ecclesiastes 5:10

13. Mark 4:18-19

14. 1 Timothy 6:17

15. Hebrews 13:5

16. Exodus 20:17

17. Luke 16:14

18. "Charles Ponzi," Notable Names Database [http://www.nndb.com/people/504/000179964/]

19. "Ponzi Scheme," Investopedia.com [http://www.investopedia.com/terms/p/ponzi-scheme.asp]

20. "Charles Ponzi," Notable Names Database [http://www.nndb.com/people/504/000179964/]

21. "In Ponzi We Trust," Smithsonian.com [http://www.smithsonianmag.com/people-places/In-Ponzi-We-Trust.html]

22. Ecclesiastes 1:9

23. "In Madoff Scandal, Jews Feel an Acute Betrayal," *The New York Times*. [http://www.nytimes.com/2008/12/24/us/24jews.html]

NON-NEGOTIABLE
NUMBER TWO

I MUST ALIGN **MY BELIEFS** WITH GOD'S **WORD** TO PRODUCE BEHAVIORS THAT WILL MAKE ME **TRULY** RICH.

CHAPTER FOUR: ROOTS ARE BELIEFS

THE ONLY SIGNIFICANCE OF LIFE CONSISTS IN HELP-
ING TO ESTABLISH THE KINGDOM OF GOD; AND THIS
CAN BE DONE ONLY BY MEANS OF THE ACKNOWLEDG-
MENT AND PROFESSION OF THE TRUTH BY EACH ONE
OF US.

– LEO TOLSTOY

Paul warned Timothy that idolizing money is only the beginning. It will lead to more and different kinds of sin. Remember those feeder roots, constantly branching out, seeking sustenance for our selfish desires?

> *Those who want to get rich fall into temptation and a trap
> and into many foolish and harmful desires that plunge people into
> ruin and destruction. For the love of money is a root of all kinds of
> evil. Some people, eager for money, have wandered from the faith
> and pierced themselves with many griefs.*[1]

Scientists have long been amazed at the incredible force that roots are able to exert on an obstacle in their way. If you've ever had one invade your septic pipes, you know what I'm talking about. Inside the root is a powerful biological system or mechanism that drives the root on.

In Paul's warning to Timothy, he describes the love of money as a root. What drives this root? The mechanism inside, if you will, is our system of beliefs reinforcing the drive to obtain what we love.

Beliefs are the key to your behavior, particularly your beliefs about money. If your beliefs are not firmly grounded in God's financial principles, you are defenseless against any false teaching that comes your way, and there is plenty of that. You will also fail to grasp the biblical definition of true riches.

Beliefs and Fruit

Our primary and feeder roots are driven by what we believe, what we think is true. Like real roots, they are crucial for producing fruit. What we believe determines the type of fruit we bear. The Me Tree, with its corrupted beliefs, cannot yield good fruit.

The Me Tree, however, will never admit this. It believes its fruit is good and it tries to convince others that its fruit is healthy, succulent and sweet. It will do all it can to show an unblemished outer skin, but the flesh within is riddled with disease. The Me Tree can never produce good fruit because it's controlled by its beliefs and seeks what it loves.

Jesus warned us about Me Trees in the language of His day:

> *Watch out for false prophets. They come to you in sheep's clothing, but inwardly they are ferocious wolves. By their fruit you will recognize them.*[2]

Let's look at another picture of the Me Tree. Its fruit might also be described as behaviors. There's a wide variety, but they all taste the same—bitter.

- The Me Tree is greedy and selfish; it hoards, storing up treasures on earth.

- The Me Tree is prideful and impressed with all it possesses; it is arrogant and seeks to impress others and be exalted.

- The Me Tree is self-indulgent and lives for its own comfort; it enjoys gambling and accumulates debt.

- The Me Tree works so that it might one day retire into leisure.

- The Me Tree has fewer children because it believes children cost too much and cramp its lifestyle.

- The Me Tree is easily corrupted; it lies, practices bribery and steals.

- The Me Tree is preoccupied with its net worth; it envies the possessions of others.

- The Me Tree covets what others have and will stop at nothing to get what it wants.

The **Me** Tree

A. W. Tozer, in his classic work, *The Pursuit of God*, described the seriousness of our problem this way:

> Our woes began when God was forced out of His central shrine and *things* were allowed to enter. Within the human heart *things* have taken over. Men have now by nature no peace within their hearts, for God is crowned there no longer, but therein the moral dusk, stubborn and aggressive usurpers fight amongst themselves for first place on the throne. This is not a mere metaphor, but an accurate analysis of our real spiritual trouble. There is within the human heart a tough, fibrous root of fallen life whose nature is to possess, always to possess. It covets things with a deep and fierce passion. The pronouns *my* and *mine* look innocent enough in print, but their constant and universal use is significant. They express the real nature of the old Adamic man better than a thousand volumes of theology could do. They are verbal symptoms of our deep disease. The roots of our hearts have grown down deep into things, and we dare not pull up one rootlet lest we die. Things have become necessary to us, a development never originally intended. God's gifts now take the place of God, and the whole course of nature is upset by this monstrous substitution.[3]

Our roots, hidden beneath the surface, are what we believe, but up above the ground, that's the fruit of our belief system. Again, what we believe controls our behavior.

Behavioral Problems Are Belief Problems

Look at 1 Timothy 6:10 again: *"For the love of money is a root of all kinds of evil."*

If the roots of the Me Tree are not changed, it won't matter how well this tree tries to behave. It won't matter how much gold or silver or net worth this tree has, its fruit is evil. Not my words, but God's. The verse doesn't say this is silly fruit, or misguided fruit. It says it's *evil*.

When I first realized the weight of that statement, it was

like a smack upside the head. Evil is the fruit produced by roots that grow in the soil of the world. Why? Because separated from God, that's all the Me Tree's roots can produce.

The Me Tree perfectly describes what I saw looking in the mirror. I saw myself with those corrupt roots embedded in my heart, taking hold and strangling my life. I had been deceived, even as a Christian. I was being conformed into the image of a Me Tree.

Disgusted and repulsed by what I had become, I swallowed hard, humbled myself, and asked God to forgive me. That repentance changed everything. My beliefs—my roots—were radically transformed.

The Self-Made Me Tree

The Me Tree loves anything that lifts up the self: *self*-help, *self*-determination, *self*-empowerment, *self*-actualization and *self*-accomplishment. It gets caught up in philosophies of self-exaltation. In America, it's impressive to hear someone say, "He's a millionaire." But do you know what we like even better? To hear, "He's a self-made millionaire." "He's rich. He's successful. And he did it all by himself."

Discerning Christians know that the Church has its share of Me Trees posing as evangelists. Far too many believers are deceived by them and become devoted disciples. But the world has its own capable "evangelists" and its own ardent disciple makers. These Me Trees feed on success stories, particularly of the self-help variety. We can all get caught up in those. We start to daydream about how we might write our own big success story to impress the other Me Trees.

One of the world's "evangelists" was George Barnard Shaw, the famous English playwright, atheist, and let's throw in *social-ist*, for good measure. Shaw said, "It is the *lack* of money that is the root of all evil."

While researching this book, I stumbled upon that quote and had to laugh at the irony of a socialist lamenting the lack of money. Perhaps he meant the lack of *someone else's money*, but I digress.

So Shaw argued that the *lack* of money was the cause of greed, corruption, pride, sloth, gluttony, etc., etc. I thought, "No way! How could anyone fall for that lie?" But do you realize that a lot of us fall for that? We get caught up in the belief that life is better with *more*. Remember Johnny Rocco? *"Yeah. That's it. More . . . I want more!"* If we could just have a little *More!* If there's a lack (and there always is), it's wrong and must be corrected. It's just that belief, as stated by the eloquent George Bernard Shaw, that enslaves so many of us.

Have you ever read, *Rich Dad, Poor Dad*?

The author, Robert Kiyosaki, is another Me Tree evangelist. His book has a catchy title and a clever tale. I kept it on my nightstand with all my other self-help material for nightly feedings back before my transformation. I've got whole pages of this book underlined!

Rich Dad, Poor Dad has sold millions and millions of copies. In fact, a dozen years after its release, it still ranks among the top on Amazon's bestseller list in the personal finance category.

Here's a nugget from one of the all-time most popular books about money: "I believe that each of us has a financial genius within us. The problem is, our financial genius lies asleep."

Wake up! That's all the Me Tree needs. Its inner genius is just asleep, and it needs to awaken so the poor Me Tree can have *More!*

Kiyosaki goes on to explain why our little financial genius is snoring away. "It lies asleep because our culture has educated us into believing that the love of money is the root of all evil."

Now that kind of talk is milk and honey to the roots of the Me Tree. No wonder the book sold millions. I would argue, however, that our culture has educated us into believing exactly the opposite, that the love of money is the root of all good.

To be fair, Kiyosaki is dead on with his description of other financial experts:

> There are many people in the world of money and finances and investments who have absolutely no idea what they are talking about. Most people in the money industry are just spouting off sales pitches. . . .

The point is that the philosophies of the world have hijacked the field of personal finance. As a result, there's such a dearth of biblical knowledge about money that even Christians operate as if they know more than God on the topic.

I told you that beliefs dictate behavior. Many of the world's evangelists believe this, too, so they harp on learning new behaviors that will help the Me Tree get rich. Here's the problem. Changing your behavior won't solve anything if you're still in bondage. The Me Tree might learn a new dance, but his love of money still calls tune.

Now, the Me Tree can always do a little pruning to improve his appearance without changing anything else. He can learn to live on a budget, to save money, and to grow his net worth. In fact, he can get filthy rich, richer than all the other Me Trees. He can even make the *Forbes'* list of billionaires, but it won't matter, because those diseased roots are still lurking just below the surface, infecting all he does because they are driven by flawed beliefs.

...There's such a dearth of biblical knowledge about money that even Christians operate as if they know more than God on the topic.

Are We Christian Humanists?

Humanism has many definitions, but I'll give you mine: It's a thought system that exalts the knowledge of man over the wisdom of God. Humanism runs rampant today, so much so that we accept it as the norm in many fields of study. Obviously, all, or nearly all of the sciences are bound by humanism, but so is financial teaching.

We're training people to become Me Trees. Many financial teachers would have you believe that sound financial *behaviors* are all you need for success in this world. You know what? They're right.

In Luke 16, Jesus tells the story of the Rich Man and Lazarus. The rich man had it all, big house, fancy clothes (no shiny cars back then), and lots of shekels in his account down at First Jerusalem Bank and Trust. No doubt he practiced very sound financial principles to achieve his worldly success.

Long story short, the arrogant rich man dies the same day as Lazarus, the pitiful beggar he had refused to help when they were both alive. Lazarus ends up in heaven, the rich dude, quite a bit further south. Moral of the story? It's about more than sound financial principles. It's about what's in your *heart* that will pass into your *roots* and control your destiny.[4]

Me Trees completely miss this. They want to be that rich guy because they believe that having enough money will solve all of their problems. Here's the nut to take from all of this: Money does not solve financial problems. It can, however, create a whole batch of new ones. Just ask a lottery winner.

According to God's Word, a change in the root system, or the heart and mind, is the real solution to all of the Me Tree's financial problems.

More or Less?

Let me give you a simple test. If there were two doors in front of you and I said, "Pick one. You can have whatever is behind that door. I'll give you a hint. Behind Door #1 is More, and behind Door #2 is Less.

Which door did you pick?

Admit it; you really, really wanted to pick Door #1. Who wouldn't? *More* is better, right? We're programmed to believe

that, to desire more of everything. More! More! More! (Just hope it's not poison ivy behind those doors.)

In the end, it doesn't matter how financially successful the Me Tree becomes. Unless its root system is transformed and it becomes a He Tree, it will remain in bondage.

D.L. Moody once said, "It seems about the hardest thing, to get to the end of self, but when we have got to the end of self, and self is lost sight of, self-seeking and self-glory thrown aside, and Christ and His cause are uppermost in our hearts, how easy it is for God to use us."[5]

Prayer Helps

I prayed a lot when I realized I was a Me Tree. I wanted desperately to become a He Tree. If you acknowledge that you need God's intervention, pray this prayer with me:

Heavenly Father, thank You for helping me see that I have a problem.

I know I've only been dealing with the issues above the surface, not at the root level.

I'm trapped in financial bondage and only looking for a way to make my pain go away. I've avoided digging down to the sin that causes me to believe money will solve my problems.

Lord, I pray You will open my heart and strengthen me to face the corrupt beliefs that keep me in bondage.

Help me to see the wisdom in Your ways and the foolishness in mine. Help me to die to that stubborn root of Self.

Help me to be an obedient servant and a better steward of the resources You've entrusted to me.

I give you my root system, Lord, to heal and use as You will.

I pray this in Jesus' name. Amen.

DIGGING DEEPER

Chapter 4 – Roots Are Beliefs

Key Points

- Beliefs drive us to obtain what we love. Bad beliefs produce bad behaviors.

- God's financial principles are not a superior form of humanism. The hope for the Me Tree is transformation, not financial success.

- Money does not solve financial problems. Only a change of beliefs will solve the root cause of the problem.

Reflection

1. Why would a nation's increasing wealth negatively impact its birth rate?

2. Robert Kiyosaki argues that our "financial genius" lies dormant because the culture teaches us that the love of money is the root of all evil. Do you agree with Kiyosaki? Why or why not?

3. Read Matthew 7:15-17. Give an example of someone you believe is a "Me Tree evangelist" about money today. How does that person's financial teaching conflict with God's Word?

4. Read Luke 16: 19-31. Who do you identify with in this story? Do you strive to "live in luxury every day and have all of your good things in your lifetime?"

5. Do you think it's possible to say you believe something and yet behave contrary to that belief? Why or why not?

6. Name five of the fruits that the Me Tree bears. Are any of them evident in your life? If so, which ones?

7. What must occur in the life of a Me Tree in order for its behaviors to change?

8. Which door would you pick: More or Less? Do you agree with Chuck that choosing "More" is a symptom of a deeper problem? Why or why not?

9. What is Non-Negotiable No. 2?

    I must _____ my _____
    with _____ _____ to
    produce _____ that will make me
    _____ rich.

Chapter 4 Endnotes

1. 1 Timothy 6:9-10

2. Matthew 7:15-16

3. *The Pursuit of God*, A.W. Tozer, 1982, Christian Publications, pg. 22

4. I'm not supporting the doctrine of salvation by works. I'm not saying you have to be nice to get to heaven. I'm just saying that all of our worldly riches avail us nothing in the end.

5. *D.L. Moody on Spiritual Leadership*, Steve Miller, Moody Press, 2004, pg. 23

CHAPTER FIVE: GOT PHILOSOPHY?

AS A MAN THINKETH IN HIS HEART, SO IS HE.[1]

Drs. Brad and Ted Klontz are recognized as leading pioneers in the emerging field of "financial psychology." They are frequently quoted in the media about issues relating to behavioral finance, money disorders and financial health. In their book, *Mind Over Money*, we learn that they have "spent years consulting with, coaching, and counseling couples and individuals struggling with money problems."

> If we have learned anything from that experience, it's that chronic self-defeating and self-destructive financial behaviors aren't driven by our rational, thinking minds. The truth is, they stem from psychological forces that lie well outside our conscious awareness, and their roots run deep, deep into our past.[2]

The professional opinions of the authors depart from scriptural teaching and I certainly don't agree with them. It is interesting to note, however, that they also see the connection between beliefs and behaviors, going so far as to call these "psychological forces" *roots*. However, while they argue that these forces lie outside our conscious awareness, I believe the challenges we have with money are in fact controlled by our rational minds.

The Me Tree needs more than "financial psychology," especially when it serves only to provide convenient excuses for self-destructive attitudes about money.

Remember, the Me Tree can be quite prosperous from the world's perspective, all the while engaging in behaviors that damage the soul. The Me Tree, by definition, remains in bondage to the self.

The roots of our beliefs do run deep, however, and it will take the power of God's Word to convince Me Trees that they aren't, in fact, *exactly what they want to be.*

Back to Slavery

In Colossians 2:8, Paul warns us, *"See to it that no one takes you captive."* He's not talking about your physical body. God's Word warns us that we can be bound in slavery through hollow and deceptive philosophy.

What exactly is our philosophy?

Philosophy is our belief system, our worldview. It's how we process millions of bits of information that enter our brains every day. It filters our thoughts and colors our perception of the world.

Paul goes on in Colossians 2:8 to describe the kind of roots or beliefs that take humans hostage, the philosophy that depends on *"human tradition and the basic principles of this world rather than on Christ."*

> *There is no end to the false beliefs that comprise the world's philosophy.*

What is the world's philosophy? There is no end to the false beliefs that comprise the world's philosophy. We could refer back to my definition of humanism, that which exalts the knowledge of man over the wisdom of God. We could also expand it to include any belief system based on man's invention, rather than God's

Word. It is essentially making the choice to seek wisdom from the tree of the knowledge of good and evil over the tree of life.

Philosophy Matters

Vishal Mangalwadi has been described in *Christianity Today* as "India's foremost Christian intellectual." He's the author of fourteen books, including *Truth and Transformation, A Manifesto for Ailing Nations.* Chuck Colson calls *Truth and Transformation* "a tour de force from someone who sees us (the West) from the outside as well as the inside."

In his excellent work, Mangalwadi observes key differences between eastern and western cultures and asks a straightforward question:

> Why don't American women haul water and cow dung on their heads?[3]

The answer, according to Mangalwadi, has nothing to do with technology or economics. We live in the twenty-first century and modern conveniences are available in both the East and the West.

Mangalwadi contends that Indian women still carry water and cow dung on their heads because of Indian beliefs about marriage. In his country, polygamy is still practiced. Culturally, men are not required to love their wives. It is not considered morally wrong for a man to love a mistress instead of his wife or to seek the services of religious prostitutes for companionship, pleasure and even "enlightenment." Wives must compete for their husband's affection and are not inclined to ask him to carry water or cow dung, because his likely response would be to simply love another wife or "worship" a temple prostitute.

Mangalwadi believes it was the Christian belief of marriage and sexual faithfulness that fueled the rapid economic advancement of western nations.

This belief in monogamous marriage brought the couple together in such a way that the energy of the husband and

Our individual beliefs not only shape our lives, they form a culture that shapes the direction of an entire nation.

wife was harnessed into a mutual desire to solve problems and so progress was more rapid than in cultures where the husband would say, "forget it, you are on your own!"

What we *believe* affects every area of our lives and those resulting *behaviors* collectively form a *culture* that shapes a *nation*. Don't miss this key point. Our individual beliefs not only shape our lives, they form a culture that shapes the direction of an entire nation.

The Lord has His own philosophy concerning money and possessions. He goes to great lengths to make that simple financial philosophy known to us: We are to love and serve Him only, not money.

His Name Is Jealous

There's a name for God that we seldom ever use. I know I don't use it very often. That name is *Jealous*.

Sounds strange, doesn't it? When we call someone jealous, it's usually to point out a character flaw. How can something we consider bad be attributed to God, especially one of His names?

Do not worship any other god, for the Lord, whose name is Jealous, is a jealous God.[4]

Back in the late 1960s, there was a popular TV western series called *The Guns of Will Sonnet*. Walter Brennan (of all people) played the title role, a Scripture-quoting man with a reputation for unparalleled gun fighting skills. As the series progressed, viewers saw the wise old man avoid more gunfights than he got into with a simple, truthful statement about his abilities: *"No brag, just fact."*

God has the title of *Jealous* because He's the only one worthy of *all* our affection and adoration. No brag, just fact.

This complete worthiness of ultimate praise grants Him and Him alone the right to be the Jealous One. He's God Almighty. He's at the top of all Kings, all Lords, all gods and all things. So jealousy is normative, if you're God.

So we understand *how* God is a righteously Jealous God, but *why* is He jealous for our adoration? It is because He loves us and knows that it's harmful for us to love anyone or anything else above Him.

In the United States, we (half) jokingly say that the golden rule is "whoever has the most gold, makes the rules." Unfortunately, there's more truth than jest in that one-liner because we tend to feel less significant than those who are more successful at acquiring wealth.

Because The Jealous One knows that the accumulation of money and possessions has the power to control our lives, He seeks to keep our heart close to His so that we will not wander off like sheep to become lunch for wolves.

In *Money and Power,* Jacques Ellul, the renowned French theologian, underscores the seriousness of this spiritual battle for our affections. He focuses on Jesus' teaching on the profound decision we all must make:

> *No servant can serve two masters. Either he will hate the one and love the other, or he will be devoted to the one and despise the other. You cannot serve both God and Money.*[5]

Love God or Love Money

Ellul contends that Jesus is warning us that money is a power unto itself—not because of what it can do, but because of what it is, intrinsically. Money is a power that can become our personal master, just as God can, and possesses a reality all its own.

Why would Jesus use the word *love* to describe our submission to money? Ellul, an eminent scholar of ancient Hebrew and Greek, says we must understand the biblical meaning of the word:

> We must be careful not to take love to mean a rather vague sentiment…love, in the Bible is utterly totalitarian . . . it involves the whole person and binds the whole person without distinction. Love reaches down into the roots of human beings and does not leave them intact.[6]

Ellul says that our love for money can become a paramount relationship in our lives, one in which we attach ourselves to money's fate. Jesus said it like this:

> *For where your treasure is, there your heart will be also.*[7]

It is vitally important, Ellul contends, that we understand the utter totality of our decision to love money and to become free of it.

> Ultimately, we follow what we have loved the most intensely either into eternity or into death. To love money is to be condemned to follow it in its destruction, its disappearance, its annihilation and its death. It is thus extremely important that we never try to justify, however little, an attachment to money or the importance we attribute to it. Nowhere are Christians told that their love for money justifies it or causes it to be used to God's glory or elevates it toward the Good. The exact opposite is said: that our attachment to money pushes us with it headlong into nothingness.[8]

Been there, done that. Recall how I justified my love of money because of all the wonderful things God could do with me once I had a lot of it. You see how it's essential that our philosophies are consistent with God's Word? If they're not, we are at risk of being enslaved by the spiritual power of money.

Into the Forest of Me Trees

My brother, John, experienced a much different outcome with his financial endeavors than did I. With skill in finance and years of experience in venture capital, his investments have resulted in more wins than losses. Much to his credit, John acknowledges that the abundance entrusted to him has come from God.

He shared with me that as he accumulated wealth, people started attributing *brilliance* to him as well as affluence. He said, "I wasn't any smarter after I had money than before, but people thought I was smarter. I'm the same person as I was before the financial success."

In Psalm 49:16, David wrote: *"Do not be overawed when a man grows rich; when the splendor of his house increases."*

I had an experience shortly after joining Crown Financial Ministries that demonstrated the practical truth of this verse.

My wife and I were invited to a party hosted at one of the biggest houses we had ever visited in our entire lives. And we're from Texas! It was hard not to walk around with our mouths open in wonder. The massive home had a three-story wood paneled library with one of those ladders that slide back and forth from floor to ceiling. The house was full of rare books and art. It had a bowling alley and a baseball field, and—and—and—well, you get the picture. This Texas-sized mansion was unbelievably impressive . . . to me.

Ann and I were driving away after the very nice party and I was still overawed, thinking our house was like a servant's quarters compared to the home we had just seen. It's easy to start comparing yourself and feeling not so rich or successful or significant. That was happening inside my mind, and I was sure Ann was going through a similar feeling.

After a brief silence, I said, "Well, Honey, what did you think?"

She looked puzzled and asked, "About what?"

Guess who was *not* overawed?

I said, "About the house. The mansion. The *MEGA*-mansion. What did you think about *it*?"

"Oh, that," Ann replied, dismissing my enthusiasm. "Do you know what I was really thinking while we were in that house?" She certainly had my attention now.

"I was thinking that what God has planned for the martyrs must be magnificent. If man can build that, think of the mansions God has built for those who love Him."

My wife recognized the fleeting nature of what man calls wealth. She understood that mere wealth pales in comparison to the true riches that last for eternity.

Then, as she often does, Ann quoted the perfect verse:

> *This is what the Lord says, "Let not the wise man boast of his wisdom or the strong man boast of his strength or the rich man boast of his riches, but let him who boasts boast of this: that he understands and knows Me, that I am the Lord, who exercises kindness, justice and righteousness on earth for in these I delight,"* declares the Lord.[9]

Luck is for Losers

I once led a Bible study attended by six couples who lived in Dallas's most expensive neighborhood. At one memorable session, the wife of a successful corporate lawyer said she felt that they *"did not have as much as other couples in their neighborhood."*

The woman said this with a tinge of bitterness in her voice. She obviously *wanted more* than her very wealthy peers.

She went on, to her husband's embarrassment, telling the entire group that every week she pins her hopes for a financial windfall on "six lucky numbers." She admitted to buying a lottery ticket in hopes of striking it rich in order to keep pace with her neighbors. She was obviously controlled by an upscale version of "Keeping Up With the Jones."

Besides the error in her judgment, I should mention here that I don't believe in random luck, karma, or that anything in the world is outside of God's sovereign control. Proverbs 16:33

says, *"The lot is cast into the lap, but its every decision is from the Lord."*

Despite everyone's discomfort (but hers), it was a "teachable moment." As gently as possible, I shared with her that this plan was a terrible idea, as her husband quietly nodded his head in agreement. I explained that gambling, and lotteries in particular, are for those who are mathematically challenged. Let me prove it.

Researchers have determined that a person who drives 10 miles to buy a lottery ticket is three times more likely to be killed in a car accident while driving to buy the ticket than he is to win the jackpot. Yet,

The odds of matching all six numbers in the Powerball Lottery are estimated to be 1 in 195,249,054.[10]

even with nearly impossible odds of ever winning a dime, one out of every four Americans *believes* their best chance of getting rich is by playing the lottery.

The Bible aptly describes those who are willing to put common sense aside in the pursuit of wealth:

> *People who want to get rich fall into temptation and a trap and into many foolish and harmful desires that plunge men into ruin and destruction.*[11]

There is a danger in interpreting this verse too narrowly, assuming that it applies only to business failures, financial losses or economic disasters. The warning covers financial *success* as well.

The "Powerball Curse"

The Powerball Lotto is a legalized multi-state form of gambling in the United States that pays enormous jackpots to the very few who purchase winning tickets.

Jack Whittaker won almost $315 million in 2002. Hardly a rags to riches story, Whittaker had plenty of money before his big win, having built a $100 million equipment company from scratch.

At first, things went well. Whittaker tithed on his winnings and was generous to a variety of charities. He reportedly gave a home, automobile and $40,000 in cash to the woman who sold him the ticket.

All of his philanthropy, however, was not enough to curb Whittaker's destructive behavior. Within a few years, he had been robbed, involved in sex scandals, bounced checks at casinos, and named in several lawsuits. The worst was still to come. He is reported to have given his teenage granddaughter a $4,000 a week allowance. Whittaker received his worst blow when the girl, perhaps the person he loved most in the world, was found dead from an apparent drug overdose.[12] The cause of all his troubles, claims Whittaker, was the "Powerball curse."

A Picture in *The Wall Street Journal*

It is not hard to see that sudden wealth can lead to a sudden downfall when it's in the hands of someone with a gambling mentality. Living only to acquire more, however, is an equally foolish proposition, even for those who are legitimately successful in their financial endeavors. The story of a dear friend's father brings this point home in a profound way.

My friend grew up in a modest home with a father who worked diligently to provide for his family. Over the years, he worked long days and most evenings. His business required him to have appointments with potential clients after most people had finished their workday. His honesty, diligence and skill allowed him to get out of debt and provide a comfortable life-style for his wife and three children.

Early in the father's career, he purchased a small lot over-looking a beautiful lake. To avoid extravagance, he conservatively moved a simple mobile home on the lot and had a deck installed around it so he could sit and watch the sunset. The family spent most weekends together at the lake as the children were growing up.

Over the years, the small business grew and so did the demands on his time. He was less able to spend time with the family as mergers and acquisitions increased the size of the company. His circle of friends changed with his success, and he found himself developing friendships with other driven businessmen. The children began to consider him distant and uninvolved in their lives. Still, he continued his relentless accumulation of more and more assets.

In a final acquisition, his company was acquired by a major publicly traded company. That landed his picture on the front page of *The Wall Street Journal*, but then disaster struck. He had traveled so very far up the ladder of financial success only to learn shortly thereafter that he had a rare disease that would take his life in a matter of weeks.

Before my friend's father died, he uttered heart-felt words summarizing the vanity of all that he had acquired. "I was happiest when sitting on the deck outside the trailer watching the sun set on the lake. I never needed anything more than that."

The Bible constantly reminds us that life on earth is fleeting, like a vapor.

> *For the sun rises with scorching heat, and it withers the plant. Its blossoms fall, and its beauty is destroyed. In the same way, the rich man will fade away while he goes about his business.*[13]

This doesn't mean that wealth is bad, only that wealth cannot shield us from the troubles of this world. God's Word gives us plenty of advance warning that no matter how much success, security or significance we attain in this world, all of it is temporal, even for kings, princes, generals, and the rich.

> *Then kings of the earth, the princes, the generals, the rich, the mighty, and every slave and every free man hid in caves and among the rocks and of the mountains. They called to the mountains and the rocks, "Fall on us and hide us from the face of him who sits on the throne and from the wrath of the Lamb!"*[14]

So you see, the Me Tree will go into hiding when the Lord returns. Regardless of his power or possessions, he will not be protected. He will feel weak and vulnerable because, finally, he understands the danger he faces.

Clear and Present Danger

While Revelation gives us a picture of what is to come at some hazy point in the future, Jesus warned the Me Trees of His day, the temple leaders, that judgment could come at any moment.

> *The ax is already at the root of the trees, and every tree that does not produce good fruit will be cut down and thrown into the fire.*[15]

The ax is already at the root of the tree.

Now, if you were a tree, what two things would you fear most? Think about it. In a single verse, the Lord warned the Pharisees that the ax is about to fall on them and they're headed for the fire. Ax and fire in one verse. Matthew 3:10 is intended to get our attention.

The Lord intended these words to frighten us to our senses. He wanted us to think, "Wow! I don't want to be that tree! What are my options?"

There is only one: repentance. You must escape the grip of money and become the kind of tree that bears good fruit. In other words, a He Tree.

Maybe you're not a Me Tree. The odds are pretty good that you know one, however. We all do, and we should feel compassion for them, because we know what lies in their path.

As Leo Tolstoy stated, "Materialists mistake that which limits life for life itself."[16]

Me Trees need to be liberated. They need redemption. They need our compassion and knowledge of the truth.

Not only is the Me Tree in clear and present danger itself, but it's also a danger to others due to its deceptive example and powerful influence.

With Me Trees growing all around us, the perceived beauty and strength of this species becomes the role model of the culture. We belong to families or live in communities or work in occupations where becoming a Me Tree is the definition of financial success. Me Trees grow and proliferate all around us. We live in a forest of Me Trees, but the danger is we can't see the forest for the trees!

Me Trees and End Times

When the Me Trees and their philosophy finally take over the entire forest, we'll know that the end times are approaching.

> But mark this: There will be terrible times in the last days. . . .[17]

Most of us picture terrible times as war, famine, disease, earthquakes, global warming, you name it. Notice, however, that Paul goes on to perfectly describe the roots of the Me Tree as terrible:

> *People will be lovers of themselves, lovers of money, boastful,*
> *proud, abusive, disobedient to their parents, ungrateful, unholy,*
> *without love, unforgiving, slanderous, without self-control, bru-*
> *tal, not lovers of the good, treacherous, rash, conceited, lovers of*
> *pleasure rather than lovers of God. . . .*[18]

Essentially, Paul is saying that the world will become over-populated with Me Trees. The Me Tree is controlled by what it loves and if left in its present condition, it will follow its love all the way to death and destruction.

The disciples asked Jesus directly when to expect the end times, and He responded:

> *Now, learn this lesson from the fig tree. As soon as its twigs*
> *get tender and its leaves come out, you know that summer is here.*[19]

No one knows the day or the hour, but we'll be able to read the signs and know when it's close:

> *Even so, when you see all these things, it is near; it's right at*
> *the door.*[20]

What things is Jesus talking about? These things are the disastrous beliefs and behaviors of the people. Jesus is saying, "Watch the people; watch what they love." When they love self and pleasure and things, this philosophy will overtake the world and eradicate love. That will be the final disaster.

> *Because of the increase of wickedness, the love of most will*
> *grow cold.*[21]

When the trees that love the world and pleasure and money have spread their fruit throughout the world, that will be our sign.

What a horrible, horrible day. The culture becomes "every man for himself" or "survival of the fittest." Darwinism gives full birth to the selfish pride of a world that denies God's existence and reaps the fruit of their deception. Everybody will be grabbing, gobbling, coveting, cheating, stealing and lying, all to get more at any cost and calling it a successful life.

DIGGING DEEPER

Chapter 5 – Got Philosophy?

Key Points

- We can all be taken captive and enslaved by the world's philosophy.
- What we believe determines the course of our lives and shapes the entire culture of our nation.
- The creeping disaster of adopting the world's philosophy is a key indicator of the End Times.

Reflection

1. Read and discuss Jacques Ellul's profound insight into the power of money:

   "Ultimately, we follow what we have loved the most intensely either into eternity or into death. To love money is to be condemned to follow it in its destruction, its disappearance, its annihilation and its death. It is thus extremely important that we never try to justify, however little, an attachment to money or the importance we attribute to it. Nowhere are Christians told that their love for money justifies it or causes it to be used to God's glory or elevates it toward the Good. The exact opposite is said: that our attachment to money pushes us with it headlong into nothingness."

2. Read Colossians 2:8. List at least one way you have been a "financial slave," taken captive by the world's philosophy?

3. Read Psalm 49:16. How does David's insight contradict the world's philosophy?

4. Read 2 Timothy 3:1. Have you marked Paul's words and kept them in the forefront of your mind to discern the danger of the world's powerful system?

5. Would you say that your worldview is biblical? In a nutshell, how would you define it?

6. What do you think Vishal Mangalwadi's assertion that a culture's beliefs about marriage affect its economic progress?

7. How does knowing that God calls Himself "Jealous" make you feel? Why do you think this attribute of God's character is often overlooked?

8. Name four things that really impress you. Which of them is the longest lasting?

9. How can a Me Tree be both a danger to itself and to others?

10. Write Non-Negotiable No. 2 in the space below.

Chapter 5 Endnotes

1. Proverbs 23:7 (KJV)

2. *Mind Over Money*, Klontz & Klontz, Broadway Books, pg. 4

3. *Truth and Transformation, A Manifesto for Ailing Nations*, Vishal Mangalwadi, YWAM Publishing, 2009, pg. 51

4. Exodus 34:14

5. Luke 16:13

6. *Money and Power*, Jacques Ellul, Wipf and Stock Publishers, 2009, pg. 83

7. Matthew 6:21

8. Op. Cit., Ellul, pg. 83

9. Jeremiah 9:23-24

10. e-How.com [http://www.ehow.com/how_5531977_calculate-odds-winning-powerball-lottery.html]

11. 1 Timothy 6:9

12. "No Fairy Tale Life for Lottery Winner," *USA Today*, Dec. 12, 2004 [http://www.usatoday.com/news/nation/2004-12-22-lottery-tragedy_x.htm]

13. James 1:11

14. Revelation 6:15-16

15. Matthew 3:10

16. *In His Image*, Brand and Yancey, Zondervan Publishers, 1984

17. 2 Timothy 3:1

18. 2 Timothy 3:2-4

19. Matthew 24:32

20. Matthew 24:33

21. Matthew 24:12

CHAPTER SIX: RICH TOWARDS GOD

BUT SATAN NOW IS WISER THAN OF YORE, AND
TEMPTS BY MAKING RICH, NOT MAKING POOR.
— ALEXANDER POPE

Money and love are often mixed together by Me Trees. Business tycoon Rajesh Jethpuria of Bhopal, India, installed an ATM in his home so his shopaholic wife would never run out of money. He explained: "It was my unique way of expressing my love. It means she never has to go to the bank and I have somewhere very secure to keep our cash."[1]

So often, when we start out using money for good, it becomes a tool for all sorts of evil. Think about the root system of the Me Tree again.

What is it that motivates it and propels it to behave this way? It's love. The Me Tree is just doing what it *loves*. And love is a great motivator. Love activates our wants and desires.

We all want more of what we love.

When I was young and single, I thought marriage was a weird idea. In fact, I equated marriage to bondage.

Marriage = bondage. Single = freedom.

Then one day in a college accounting class, I got to talking with a beautiful girl who sat in front of me. Eventually, I offered her a ride home. In the days that followed, I gradually got to know Ann and before I knew it, I was deeply in love with her. In just a few weeks, I went from thinking marriage was dumb to believing it was the greatest idea ever conceived. Marriage was no longer bondage; it was the means to be with Ann for the rest of my life. My beliefs changed because I wanted more of what I loved. And when my beliefs changed, so did my behaviors.

This principle applies to every living person. When the Me Tree *loves* the things of this world, it naturally wants more of them. Love motivates it and forms its beliefs. In doing so, love of money and possessions comes to control the Me Tree.

Mother Teresa said, "Everybody seems to be in such a terrible rush; anxious for greater developments and greater riches, and so on, so that children have little time for their parents, and parents have little time for each other. And in the home begins the disruption of peace of the world."[2]

She observed that people want more of everything and that our love for possessions and significance is greater than our love for the people in our lives. Things meant almost nothing to her, and she was able to recognize this perverse behavior all around her.

Aleksandr Solzhenitsyn, the great Russian novelist, made a similar observation when he addressed the 1978 graduating class at Harvard University:

> . . . The constant desire to have still more things and a still better life and the struggle to obtain them imprints many Western faces with worry and even depression... it has become possible to raise young people according to these ideals, leading them to physical splendor, happiness, possession of material goods, money and leisure, to an almost unlimited freedom of enjoyment. . . .
>
> Even biology knows that habitual extreme safety and well-being are not advantageous for a living organism. Today, well-being in the life of Western society has begun to reveal its pernicious mask.[3]

Mother Teresa identified the love of earthly riches in the Me Tree. Solzhenitsyn identified the Me Tree's love of comfort and pleasure. Left unchanged, that love becomes a trap that can snare any one of us.

Strongholds

The word *stronghold* is used two ways in the Bible. Often, it describes something quite positive.

> *The Lord is a refuge for the oppressed, a stronghold in times of trouble.*[4]

> *The Lord is my rock, my fortress, my deliverer; my God is my rock, in whom I take refuge. He is my shield and the horn of my salvation, my stronghold.*[5]

At other times, the word stronghold is used in a negative sense:

> *For the weapons of our warfare are not of the flesh but have divine power to destroy strongholds.*[6]

In this passage from 2 Corinthians, Paul refers to a spiritual *stronghold* that resists God's truth and must be destroyed. The Me Tree views his wealth and possessions as a source of protection, a fortress, but in reality, his stronghold is a prison in which he is held captive.

It's difficult to escape from something you think is your security and protection. Abandoning its stronghold to walk in freedom makes no sense to the Me Tree who only finds peace with his material possessions. *"I need all of those things! Do you expect me to live without security and protection in life?"*

If money is our source of security, we have locked ourselves inside a prison of our own making. We willingly remain in captivity unless we find security and protection somewhere else.

What we love the most we also have the most fear of losing. If we fear losing money because it is our security, we give Satan the power to control us and keep us captive.

More than that, the love of self, money and pleasure is spiritually *deadly* because it prevents our hearts from moving toward the only real sanctuary, the fortress Jesus Christ.

Fear of Loss

I have seen Christians terrified of the Great Recession. I've seen Christians panicked because their homes have lost value. I've seen Christians who thought the world was coming to an end because the stock market plunged, taking much of retirement savings down with it. I've seen Christians scared to death when they experience even the smallest financial loss. They cry out in fear because their source for security is threatened. What they're really saying is, *"My fortress is crumbling."*

Remember Bernie Madoff? His scam was built upon a sense of guaranteed returns. Madoff was a master con artist, the greatest of our time, but he wasn't the first, or the most successful. For centuries Christians and non-Christians alike have been duped into believing a similar scam, pulled off by no less than the Devil himself, that earthly riches guarantee us safety and protection. We have happily entered his fortress and kept ourselves locked inside. The question becomes, when will we realize we're being scammed? Will it be early enough to do something about it, or after it's too late, as was the case with Bernie Madoff's victims?

The question becomes, when will we realize we're being scammed?

I read many of the news stories about Madoff's victims. I feel compassion for those who were deceived and ripped off, left without their life savings to carry them through retirement. It was a tragic crime of epic proportions. I also noted a common sentiment of those who lost their money in his scam. It went something like this, *"I hope he goes straight to hell."* Do not pass go; do not collect $200. Just go straight to hell. Not a hint of forgiveness.

While I didn't really expect Madoff's victims to feel sympathy for him after the evil he committed, I was still surprised by the intensity of their hatred for the man who took their money. They were angry because he stole what they loved. He stole their stronghold, what they had inherited or worked hard to accumulate. He stole their source of security. So, as far as they were concerned, just send the guy to *hell*. Jail was too nice for him.

Fear of loss is a key indicator to determine if you are in love with things. James 5:1-5 shouts another early warning, indicating that we should not lock ourselves inside the fortress of wealth.

> *Now listen, you rich people. Weep and wail because of the misery that's coming upon you. Your wealth has rotted, and moths have eaten your clothes. Your gold and silver are corroded. Their corrosion will testify against you and eat your flesh like fire. You've hoarded wealth in the last days, and the cries of the harvesters have reached the ears of the Lord Almighty. You have lived on earth in luxury and self-indulgence, and you have fattened yourself in the day of slaughter.*

Just as the *love* of money, not money itself, is the root of all kinds of evil, James is not saying that it's wrong simply to possess wealth. I certainly am not saying that, either. Wealth, earthly wealth, can be a very good thing if it's used the right way by someone who understands where it comes from. Without surplus wealth, there wouldn't be much progress. We wouldn't have police, firefighters, hospitals or schools. Without surplus wealth, we wouldn't even have church buildings, so please, don't misconstrue what I'm saying to mean that rich people are "bad."

We do have a choice with regard to riches, however. We can become rich towards self, piling up treasure in our fortresses of false security, or we can become rich towards God, the only real source of protection. This is the war being waged in every soul.

Grace for Stumps

> Everybody can be great . . . because anybody can serve.
> You don't have to have a college degree to serve. You don't have
> to make your subject and verb agree to serve. You only need a
> heart full of grace. A soul generated by love.[7]
>
> — Martin Luther King Jr.

King Nebuchadnezzar thought he had it all. He was the ruler of the most powerful kingdom in the world. Comparatively, his power was on par with the greatest empires in the history of mankind.

At the pinnacle of his reign, this great king had a dream. He dreamed he was a Me Tree. Well, that's not exactly how it goes in your Bible, so please allow me a little literary license.

Nebuchadnezzar dreamed that as a Me Tree, he had grown very large, indeed.[8] But as his dream progressed, the king learned that he was going to get cut down, way down, all the way down to a stump right at ground level. Sounds more like a nightmare to me!

At first glance, this sounds terrible, but God would eventually shed his grace on the "stump king." Before we get to that, let's take a look at what brought the powerful despot down.

A year after the dream, Nebuchadnezzar was walking on the roof of the royal palace of Babylon, surveying his vast accomplishment with pride. He said, *"Is not this the great Babylon I have built as the royal residence, by my mighty power and for the glory of my majesty?"*[9]

That Me Tree was very impressed with himself, wasn't he? His roots were swollen with self-love. Shortly after his attitude is revealed, in his moment of shining self-glory, whack! The Me Tree gets cut down and becomes a stump.

God essentially had forewarned Nebuchadnezzar that he was going to become a stump. Where's the grace, you ask? By leaving the stump in the ground and not killing it, God preserved Nebuchadnezzar's roots so that the king would be able to grow back into a new kind of tree.

God said, *"Seven times will pass by for you until you acknowledge that the Most High is sovereign over the kingdoms of men and gives them to anyone he wishes."*[10]

God allowed the fallen king time to grow humble. By His grace, He preserved the roots of the stump until this powerful king was willing to acknowledge that God was truly in control.

There is hope for you who may feel like the fallen King Nebuchadnezzar, a stump that has lost everything dear or precious to you. Maybe you, too, feel like you've been cut down and that your circumstances are bleak. There is no need to despair or rail that you've been treated unfairly. By God's grace, you have the solution. Where is the hope for your transformation?

Romans 12 begins this way, *"Therefore, I urge you, brothers, in view of God's mercy. . . ."*[11]

God's incredible, unmerited, unlimited mercy.

Have you ever desperately needed mercy from another person? What would you have given for it? Just about anything, right? What about your children? Has one of them ever been in serious trouble and needed mercy? Weren't all your efforts focused on finding a way to spare your child?

We're all in trouble, born into this world with bad roots. So God, through the apostle Paul, clearly expressed the solution:

> *In view of God's mercy, offer yourselves as living sacrifices, holy and pleasing to God. This is your spiritual act of worship.*[12]

Every Me Tree is invited to partake of God's mercy and to offer ourselves to Him as an act of worship. We must only offer ourselves to God, saying, "Thank you for your kindness, grace and mercy. Here I am Lord, rotten roots and all. I'm yours."

Isn't that practical? But His advice continues.

> *Do not conform to the pattern of this world, but be transformed by the renewing of your mind. Then you will be able to test and approve what God's will is—his good, pleasing and perfect will.*[13]

When we offer ourselves to Him as a response to His grace, acknowledging that we have the same sinful pride as King Nebuchadnezzar, we will no longer be conformed to the pattern of this world, but we'll be *transformed by the renewing of our mind*. When our beliefs change, we change. Amazing.

If you're thinking, "That's way too easy. It'll never work," I beg to differ. I've been there; I've done it, and my experience supports my opinion. Further, every sincere follower of Christ will give testimony to the powerful reality of this transformation.

What does the Bible say controls the Me Tree and its behavior? What it believes. What it thinks. It's held captive by the philosophy of the world, but it is also transformed by faith or a change in beliefs that are exercised as one who looks to God for mercy and forgiveness of sin.

It's not self-help, but help from the Living God.

Sometimes we want to take hold of a Me Tree and just pull it up by its roots! But the Scripture doesn't say that the Me Tree has to be *transplanted*. It says it must be *transformed*. And sometimes, I think we just miss that grace. This tree, with its natural, flawed roots, full of itself, can be transformed by changing what it *believes*. That's called faith. That change comes from the outside of the tree and penetrates into the root system. It's not self-help, but help from the Living God.

Supernatural Change

Transformation as described in Romans 12 is a *super*natural change. Supernatural means that it transcends human law. That's the stuff of miracles. Miracles supersede the mere laws of nature. That's what this transformation accomplishes. The utterly undeserving Me Tree, because of God's grace, can undergo supernatural change without having its roots pulled up, trained or transplanted.

Do you want to see one of those transformed Me Trees, a person that experienced supernatural transformation by God's grace?

The man in the picture standing next to the beautiful bride is not the same man today. While I may look like the same man

(sort of), my wife Ann has witnessed the supernatural changes. I'm radically different because God's Spirit came into me and transformed me. I received no "training" to behave differently; rather, I was transformed by faith in God.

Here's the good news. It can happen to you, too. So, you can relax. Take a deep breath and rejoice in how good and kind God is, because He takes every tree just as it comes to Him. You don't have to be wealthy or successful; you don't have to study a lot of financial "how to" books. If you've been working really hard to make something of yourself in the world's view, just stop. You cannot be redeemed by financial success. You can be successful financially and still be redeemed, but your success will not redeem you. Only God can do that.

Many men and women today are just like I was; they're trying really hard to prove themselves. Their balance sheet has become their scorecard. I've met people who say things like, "I was raised poor, and I made a vow that would never happen to me again." That vow came to control their lives.

After a year in prison, Bernie Madoff gave an interview from his prison cell. He expressed a similar drive, explaining that he witnessed his father suffer a humiliating financial failure.

Madoff explained that he was so afraid of repeating his father's failure in business, of losing the honor and esteem of men, that he chose to commit a crime.

Riches can never set a man free. We're not redeemed by fame. We're not redeemed by power. We're not redeemed by how big our kingdom may be on this earth. We are only redeemed by Jesus Christ and the wonderful power of the Gospel, that miraculous transaction that takes place through faith when His life resides within us. Then, and only then, will our roots be changed.

You remember those bad roots? We said they're invisible, they're pervasive, and they're responsible for bad fruit. When the Me Tree embraces the truth of God's Word, however, it is made new through a process that cannot be explained in human terms. God's love floods into it's heart, life comes into the tree, travels down into the roots and redirects their energies from the love of self to the love of people; from the love of money to the love of God; and from the love of pleasure to the love of giving.

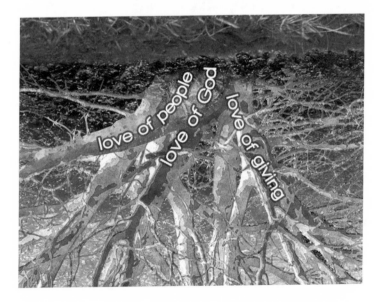

The Bible tells us over and over that our belief system (faith) gives us strength. Our behavior, what people see on the outside, is an expression of what's going on inside our hearts and minds. That's why we must diligently guard our minds and constantly renew them with truth.

> *The weapons we fight with are not the weapons of the world. On the contrary, they have divine power to demolish strongholds. We demolish arguments and every pretense that sets itself up against God, and we take captive every thought to make it obedient to Christ.*[14]

Now, this transformed tree, the He Tree, has feeder roots as well. When it's planted firmly in God's Truth, abiding in and relying on God's Word, its roots will soak up all the nutrients it needs to keep going and growing strong.

Key Indicators of the Supernatural He Tree

- **This tree believes in God's Word.**

Scripture promises advantages to this tree when it turns from the world's philosophy and feeds upon Truth.

> *Blessed is the man who walks and lives not in the counsel of the ungodly.*[15]

When we turn from the world's advice, plans and purposes, we will be *blessed*, literally meaning happy, fortunate, prosperous, and enviable, having great advantage or favor.

- **This tree believes it's more blessed to give than to receive.**

> *In everything I did, I showed you that by this kind of hard work we must help the weak, remembering the words the Lord Jesus himself said: "It is more blessed to give than to receive."*[16]

In stark contrast to the world, this is a guiding philosophy for the He Tree's use of money.

This tree does not fear, but rather has faith in God's provision.

> But seek first his kingdom and his righteousness, and all these things will be given to you as well.[17]

This tree is secure and content. It doesn't have to run after things.

- **This tree believes in serving God only.**

> No one can serve two masters. Either he will hate the one and love the other, or he will be devoted to the one and despise the other. You cannot serve both God and Money.[18]

Aware of the temptation and power of money to enslave it, this tree makes a conscious daily decision to have only one Master, God.

- **This tree believes it is small compared to God.**

> For everyone who exalts himself will be humbled, and he who humbles himself will be exalted.[19]

Understanding that pride is cancerous to its roots, it is humble.

This tree helps those whom others consider insignificant.

> Then Jesus said to his host, "When you give a luncheon or dinner, do not invite your friends, your brothers or relatives, or your rich neighbors; if you do, they may invite you back and so you will be repaid."[20]

The "poor, the crippled, the lame, and the blind" are of special interest to this tree. It believes that it will be repaid at the resurrection of the righteous for generously caring for these.

- **This tree believes in faithfulness with small things.**

> So if you have not been trustworthy in handling worldly wealth, who will trust you with true riches?[21]

It knows that God expects it to be trustworthy with handling money. Larry Burkett, the late cofounder of Crown Financial Ministries, was fond of saying, *"God tells us that money is a little bitty thing. It's a little bitty test. Pass the test."*

If you want to be trusted with much in the kingdom to come, pass the *little bitty* test. That's how you will grow truly rich. The verse promises that if you pass that test, you will experience *true riches*. Not the riches of the world; the riches of Christ available immediately and in the life to come.

- **This tree believes in eternal rewards.**

    "I tell you the truth," Jesus said to them, "no one who has left home or wife or brothers or parents or children for the sake of the kingdom of God will fail to receive many times as much in this age and, in the age to come, eternal life."[22]

- **This tree lives in hope of one day hearing, "Well done, good and faithful servant."**

    His master replied, "Well done, good and faithful servant! You have been faithful with a few things; I will put you in charge of many things. Come and share your master's happiness!"[23]

This tree longs to please its Master; therefore it's no longer controlled by the world's view of success, significance or security. It's been set free by faith in the Truth.

Fruit of the Supernatural He Tree

With its new, healthy root system, abiding and exercising faith in the Living Word, beautiful, supernatural fruit is borne from this tree.

The first is love. Not love of self and money and pleasure, but love of God and others, and the unbridled action of love called giving.

The entire law is summed up in a single command: "Love your neighbor as yourself."[24]

But there is so much more:

> *But the fruit of the Spirit is love, joy, peace, patience, kind-*
> *ness, goodness, faithfulness, gentleness and self-control. Against*
> *such things there is no law. Those who belong to Christ Jesus have*
> *crucified the sinful nature with its passions and desires. Since we*
> *live by the Spirit, let us keep in step with the Spirit.*[25]

So you see, the He Tree is wise; it's humble; it's obedient; it's
dead to the world; it's reliable; it loves children and the elderly;
it's compassionate; it's not easily offended; it's kind to the poor
and the widow; it's impartial; it's honest; it fears God; it saves for

The **He** Tree in Full Bloom

the future; it cares for the sick and visits the prisoner; it's able to persevere through trials; and it accepts temporal loss of worldly riches because it has stored its treasures in heaven.

As the He Tree is transformed, fruit starts to spring forth. The He Tree spreads out its limbs making visible the beauty, the glory and the manifest riches of Christ to be shared with the world.

Because the He Tree is loved by God, it also loves people.

> *We love because he first loved us.*[26]

The He Tree prospers in the eyes of God because its love for others bears the fruit that comes from God, not man.

> *A generous man will prosper; he who refreshes others will himself be refreshed.*[27]

Why was Paul content no matter what hardships he faced?

> *I have learned the secret of being content in any and every situation, whether well fed or hungry, whether living in plenty or in want. I can do everything through him who gives me strength.*[28]

Paul learned that our riches do not depend on physical treasure in this world, but the very real treasure of Christ that we can experience here and for eternity in heaven. This bounty of Christ's grace fills the roots of the He Tree with contentment regardless of the amount of money it may or may not possess.

If This Tree Dies, We Will All Be in Poverty.

The world will be a terrible place if the He Tree becomes extinct. Imagine how utterly destitute the planet would be without any He Trees.

The Lord planted these trees in His soil to grow among the Me Trees so that His forest would contain the priceless fruits that reveal His true riches and bounty to the world. Do you see how important it is to be a He Tree?

In 2 Timothy 3, Paul warns us to "mark his words" that Me Trees would grow and proliferate and influence others to grow in the love of money, self and pleasure. He declared that it would be a terrible day when every man lives for himself, when love of others grows cold and this fruit no longer exists. Those days will be so horrible that the Lord will use them as a sign that the end of history is near.

The Gospel must be preached to the ends of the earth. Without God's Truth to transform Me Trees into the image of Christ, into He Trees, the world will be devoid of love. That's the kind of "climate change" that really will kill everything.

The Big Issue

Can you now see the bigger economic issue of our time?

The issue is not limited to getting people out of debt so that we can experience financial freedom for our own benefit. The world is already full of materialists. The issue is not to increase our money and possessions to have financial security. The world is already full of those who trust in their bank accounts or appreciable assets. The issue is not to find joy and pleasure in the ultimate pursuit of getting rich. The world is already full of those addicted to self-fulfillment.

The issue is to become *truly* rich! This can only happen when our hearts and our entire root system are transformed completely by God's Truth. Then, and only then, can we live, grow and multiply He Trees. God has entrusted us with this world changing purpose.

A Small Glimpse

Not long ago a friend of mine called and said, "Hey, Chuck, I want to tell you a story. My wife and I set up a scholarship at a private Christian university. There was a maintenance worker there that we knew when we were in school, so we gave this gift anonymously, an academic scholarship, in the name of the maintenance worker that worked on campus for years."

I said, "Well, that's great."

There was more to the story than just my friend's generosity, however. He continued, "You see, the boy that received that scholarship, has just graduated college. He was so appreciative and grateful for that scholarship that he went to the school administration and asked for the name and address of that maintenance worker. They provided him the information, so the student called him and thanked him for providing his scholarship to the university.

"The maintenance worker was glad to receive this gratitude but replied, 'I'm getting the blessing of this, but let me tell you who really gave the money.' The humble maintenance worker told him our names, the name of the real donors."

"Great story!" I said, again thinking that was it.

"Wait, I'm not finished," my friend said, eager to tell me the final outcome.

"The young man, whose name is John, just called me, and you should know what he shared with me."

"Okay, let's hear it," I said, wondering why this story should be important to me.

"John first thanked me and my wife saying, 'I want to tell you I just graduated from the university, and I'm so grateful that your scholarship allowed me to do it. You see, my father died when I was five months old, and I couldn't have ever gone to school without your gift.'

"'Well thank you,' we told John, 'But that was just a partial scholarship we donated. How else did you make it through school?'

"'Well, years ago, an anonymous family established an educational fund for me when my father died. It was from some people that I never knew. And with your scholarship and the money in my educational fund, I graduated from this private Christian university without any debt.'"

My generous friend now turned the conversation towards me and said, "Chuck, do you know John?"

"Nope, but it's a great story and one that I can certainly share with others. Thank you for passing it along to me."

He then said, "Chuck, you and Ann established John's educational fund. You and Ann did that when he was five months old."

I was stunned. "Really? Are you kidding me?"

I had forgotten all about that little five-month-old boy. I remember his mother briefly worked for Ann, and one day after she learned that the woman was a widow, she came home and said, "This little boy doesn't have a dad. Why don't we do something?" So we opened an education account, made a donation and asked some friends to join us. Shortly after that we lost touch with the woman and her little boy.

It turned out that wasn't the end of the story. John told my friend something else. "There's one more thing I want you to know. I've applied for seminary. That's my dream, to be a pastor and serve the Lord."

The little boy I never knew would someday preach the Gospel of Jesus Christ. What a huge, unexpected repayment of our small act of generosity. I was humbled.

That wonderful reminder caused me to think that one day, all the little acts of kindness that we forget over the course of our lives, the Lord will recall. Perhaps He will say, "I remember that. I know you weren't thinking about getting repaid but I want to share the joy with you now."

I know how we're going to feel on that day. We're going to feel rich. Really, really rich.

Prayer

Heavenly Father, thank You for your Word that illuminates our minds and refreshes our thoughts. Thank You for Your wisdom that allows us to break the bonds of this world's philosophies.

Without You, Lord, they take hold of all of us because Satan never stops taking captives. Without You, we know only tension, struggle and the desire for worldly wealth.

Lord, I pray that our minds are prepared to receive more of what You want to teach us. Let us see that if our hearts long to gain temporal wealth, there is no future. Let us recognize this is a great idol, the powerful philosophy that takes more captives every day.

You've called us to know the Truth, and that Truth will set us free. Heavenly Father, I pray that You will prepare us to understand our role to plant more trees that grow in the soil of Your truth and produce the fruit that the world truly needs.

I thank You, Father, for the joy of knowing that You have planted Your trees around the world, those who love You and want to give You their very best. Thank You for the trees who love You alone with heart, soul, and mind.

I thank You in Jesus' name. Amen.

DIGGING DEEPER

Chapter 6 – Rich Towards God

Key Points

- We all want more of what we love: the desire for riches, power and pleasure are natural drivers of our behavior.

- Money is one of Satan's key strongholds that thwarts our usefulness to God's purposes.

- By God's mercy and grace, He transforms Me Trees into He Trees.

- The beliefs of the He Tree produce the behaviors that Christ wants to use to enrich the world.

- If the He Tree dies, we are all in poverty.

Reflection

1. Read Daniel 4. Give an example of a time when, like King Nebuchadnezzar, you felt that you were a stump in need of God's grace.

2. Consider Martin Luther King, Jr.'s philosophy of the essential nature of becoming great:

    "Everybody can be great . . . because anybody can serve. You don't have to have a college degree to serve. You don't have to make your subject and verb agree to serve.

You only need a heart full of grace. A soul generated by love."

How can you apply this approach to your current circumstances?

3. Read Romans 12:1-2, 2 Corinthians 10:4-5 and Psalm 1:1. Are you ready for the supernatural transformation promised by God's Word?

4. Do you agree with the statement that we love most what we fear losing most? Why or why not?

5. Explain how a stronghold can be both a place of safety and a prison.

6. What does it mean to be "rich towards God"?

7. Which characteristics of a Me Tree could make it difficult for people to accept God's mercy?

8. Try to write Non-Negotiable No. 2 from memory:

Chapter 6 Endnotes

1. The Free Library, "Tycoon's wife is in the money" [http://www.thefreelibrary.com/Tycoon's+wife+is+in+the+money%3b+Bizarre+stories+from+around+the+world%3a...-a0241436762]

2. EWTN Global Catholic Network, "Quotes of Mother Teresa" [http://www.ewtn.com/motherteresa/words.htm]

3. "A World Split Apart," Aleksandr I. Solzhenitsyn. Commencement address delivered at Harvard University, June 8, 1978. Harvard Archives: HUC 6978. 82.7 [also http://www.columbia.edu/cu/augustine/arch/solzhenitsyn/harvard1978.html]

4. Psalm 9:9

5. Psalm 18:2

6. 2 Corinthians 10:4

7. "The Drum Major Instinct" sermon, Martin Luther King Jr., www.thekingcenter.org

8. You can read the specifics of Nebuchadnezzar's vivid, detailed dream in Daniel 4.

9. Daniel 4:30

10. Daniel 4:32

11. Romans 12:1

12. Ibid.

13. Romans 12:1-2

14. 2 Corinthians 10: 4-5

15. Psalm 1:1 (AMP)

16. Acts 20:35

17. Matthew 6:33

18. Matthew 6:24

19. Luke 14:11

20. Luke 14:12

21. Luke 16:11

22. Luke 18:29-30

23. Matthew 25:23

24. Galatians 5:14

25. Galatians 5:22-25

26. 1 John 4:19

27. Proverbs 11:25

28. Philippians 4:12-13

NON-NEGOTIABLE
NUMBER THREE

I MUST **ACT** UPON AND **APPLY** SPIRITUAL
TRUTH IN ORDER TO RECEIVE TRUE RICHES.

CHAPTER SEVEN: THE ROOT OF RICHES

YET AS I READ THE BIRTH STORIES ABOUT JESUS I
CANNOT HELP BUT CONCLUDE THAT THOUGH THE
WORLD MAY BE TILTED TOWARD THE RICH AND POW-
ERFUL, GOD IS TILTED TOWARD THE UNDERDOG.
— PHILLIP YANCEY

When my oldest two sons, Hank and Todd, were small boys, we took a family vacation to the Colorado mountains with two other families. Both of the other families had far more money than the Bentleys. In my opinion, if we were to compare bank accounts at that time, theirs were probably 100 times larger than mine. Based on income or net worth, I could have been considered poor in this mix of families.

For some reason during the vacation, eight-year-old Todd became aware of this. We're not sure how this came to his attention; perhaps the other children had more options when spending their pocket money. Regardless of the reason, one morning the adults were all sitting around a table outside a café, enjoying the morning conversation over a cup of coffee when Todd appeared.

He crawled up into my lap and began tugging on my arm just as I was making some point or other with the adults. I paused and excused myself to allow my curious son to ask his question. He had my full attention and, as I would soon regret, the attention of everyone at the table. All eyes were on Todd.

"Dad, are we rich?" Todd asked matter-of-factly and loud enough for everyone to hear.

I could not believe he was asking me about such a private matter, especially in the presence of the very people who had sooo much more money than we did!

I blushed and thought about how I was going to answer him. It got very quiet around the table.

"Well, yes, Todd, we are rich."

He beamed with pride as a smile broke out across his face. I thought that would end the conversation and he would get back to playing with the other kids. He wasn't quite satisfied, though.

"How rich are we Dad?"

His eyes locked on mine and I could hear a few folks chuckling from behind their coffee mugs as they waited to see how I would handle this one. This question drew more interest than the first!

"Todd, well, uh…we are very, very, very rich." My son had to ponder this one for a few seconds. It also raised a few eyebrows on the faces of our friends who were aware of the vast difference in our incomes.

"Richer than Ross Perot?" Todd shot back.

He was not letting go now. He wanted some real answers. I have no idea how an eight-year-old even knew of Texas billionaire H. Ross Perot, or why he would want to compare our humble family with this icon of the mega-rich of Texas where we lived at the time. He was not going to let it go, however, even as I silently prayed for him to go back and play like the other good little children.

"Todd, I'm going to have to tell you the truth. Son, I don't know Ross Perot so I can't be certain, but I believe I am the richest man on the face of the earth."

"Wow!" Todd's eyes looked up and beyond into the sky as if he were trying to imagine just how vast my financial holdings might be. I let it hang there for a few seconds as everyone around the table enjoyed this spontaneous moment of intimacy between father and son. There were some quiet smiles on the faces of our friends who thought that this was finally the end of the conversation. Ann, however, was giving me a look that I knew meant, "Tell him the truth!" Perhaps I would have, but Todd had one more question before his curiosity would be satisfied.

"So, does that mean I can spend whatever I want on anything I want?" Now I finally knew what all this was about.

"No, Todd, you can't spend money on whatever you want, because our riches have nothing to do with how much money we have. I wasn't thinking about money when I answered you."

"Oh, Dad, I thought we were really rich!" he said loudly as he jumped out of my lap and headed back to playing with his friends.

Better Than Gold

Everyone got a chuckle out of this exchange, knowing that I was on the spot answering such an unexpected question in front of a group of friends. I was about to get back to the regular chitchat with the adults when one of the other men looked at me and said, "Great answer."

My friend, who had considerable money, went further. "You affirmed to him what is really true. Money and wealth are not the same."

That story has always reminded me of Proverbs 16:16, *"How much better it is to get skillful and godly wisdom than gold! And to get understanding is to be chosen rather than silver."*

He Trees are rich, richer than all Me Trees, regardless of how much money they have accumulated, because the root of riches is found in Christ.

He Trees abide in Christ and experience supernatural peace and security.

...The root of riches is found in Christ.

God promised that He will never leave them or forsake them. That promise enables the He Tree to live without fear, without constantly worrying about not having enough money, or things or status. The He Tree has already been made rich in every way in God's economy.

> You will be made rich in every way so that you can be generous on every occasion.[1]

God makes the He Tree rich in *every way* so that it will give God's riches to others, not hoarding them for itself. These marvelous riches are to be shared on *every occasion*. There should never be a fence around the He Tree to keep others away from its fruit.

The Gospel of True Riches

One day, God will pull back the curtain to reveal everyone we've loved, served and helped to liberate in our lives. These are people whom we may have unknowingly blessed because of the fruit we bore. On that day, He will say to you, "Well done. You accomplished the purpose that I planned for you. This was why I put you on earth. You didn't get trapped in the philosophy of this world and build your own kingdom. You did what I asked you to do and remained faithful."

There's more good news for the supernatural He Tree. This tree can actually handle money quite well. It can be trusted with temporal riches because it doesn't love them and its roots do not crave them.

God looks upon the transformed heart of this tree and says, "This tree can be my steward, my faithful trustee who is not controlled by worldly wealth. This tree will be one that is not deceived by money. This tree will be one that is willing to share all of My riches with the world. This tree will be one that I use for My purposes, for all eternity. Because this tree was faithful with a little, one day I will place it in charge of much more, for all time."

Just How Rich Is the He Tree?

Throughout history, men and women alike have held worldly riches in their hands. Some have been extraordinarily wealthy.

Many marvel at the vast and extravagant amounts of gold and jewels buried in the tomb of Egyptian King Tutankhamen. Some are awestruck by the extravagant beauty of the Taj Mahal; still others by the sparkle and sheer size of the Hope Diamond.

For a more contemporary example, consider the net worth of Mexican businessman Carlos Slim Helu, considered the wealthiest man alive. This 70-year-old telecom entrepreneur recently eclipsed Bill Gates for "world's richest man" status, with assets exceeding $53 billion.[2]

All very impressive, but the Bible is clear that those who experience the riches of Jesus Christ have no equals, even compared to the wealthiest the world has to offer. Christ's riches are described as *incomparable*,[3] *unsearchable*,[4] and *glorious*.[5] The adjectives used to describe His riches are never used to describe the wealth of mere men. Meditate on these passages:

> *Oh, the depth of the riches of the wisdom and knowledge of God. Oh, how unsearchable his judgments, and his paths are beyond tracing out.*[6]

> *In Him we have redemption through His blood, the forgiveness of sins in accordance with the riches of God's grace.*[7]

> *I pray also that the eyes of your heart may be enlightened in order that you may know the hope to which he has called you, the riches of his glorious inheritance in the saints.*[8]

> *And my God will meet all of your needs according to His glorious riches.*[9]

We serve the King of Kings. We serve the Owner of it All. He's the richest there ever was or ever can be. And His riches enter our lives through that mysterious process of faith, and they're stored deep in our root system. Paul said, "*God has cho-*

sen to make known among the Gentiles the glorious riches of this mystery, which is Christ in you, the hope of glory."[10]

Christ in *you*! Christ *in* the roots of your tree is the real treasure. It's not external, not you behaving and acting like a Christian. It's not you increasing your net worth by following rules or principles, but the reality of the living God coming *into* your root system and sharing His riches with you.

Solomon's Bottom Line

Solomon, the wealthiest and wisest man of his time, clearly realized that God operated from financial principles wholly apart from the world's.

Drawn from His wisdom, God's financial principles never fail, yet the foolish seek wisdom from other men. I used to be one of them. Remember my overstuffed bookcase? There must have been guys like me around in Solomon's day, which prompted him to write about the futility of men seeking knowledge from other men. He puts it this way:

> *Of making many books there is no end, and much study wearies the body.*[11]

I had wearied my mind, spirit and body seeking wisdom from the endless sources of books eager to sell me the formula to satisfy my dual desires: to get rich and be recognized as the smart fellow I thought I was. But Solomon's advice goes beyond telling us where not to look; he also reveals to us where we should look to satisfy all of our desires.

> *Now all has been heard; here is the conclusion of the matter: Fear God and keep his commandments, for this is the whole [duty] of man. For God will bring every deed into judgment, including every hidden thing, whether it is good or evil.*[12]

Solomon concisely points us to the bottom line of the matter. The final conclusion he describes as the duty of all mankind, is to fear God and keep His commandments. As simple and profound as this may seem, it took me years to agree that Solomon was right and I was wrong.

Controlled by What We Love

In the Bentley household, we have several pets. One of them is a very stubborn Welsh Corgi officially named Bella, but I prefer to call her Sassy. She's smart as a whip, loyal and a loving companion, but her independent streak at first made it impossible to train her.

Our breakthrough came when we realized that she is totally "food controlled." If there's even a hint that a treat is part of the deal, stubborn little Bella loses the "tude" and becomes a pushover. She can't help it; she was made that way and will gladly exchange obedience for food.

In the very same way, you and I are wired by God to be "love controlled." We are created to exchange our obedience for love. Since love is a matter of the heart, we are ultimately controlled by what we allow in our heart. This voluntary submission to what we love will either trap us in the world's philosophies about money or liberate us to experience true riches found only in the faithful obedience to God and His Word. The Bible makes this relationship very clear. If you love money, you will never have financial security.

> *Whoever loves money never has money enough; whoever loves wealth is never satisfied with his income.*[13]

If you love pleasure, you will never have financial success.

> *The sluggard's craving will be the death of him, because his hands refuse to work.*[14]

If you love getting instead of giving, you will never have true significance.

> *A greedy man stirs up dissension, but he who trusts in the Lord will prosper.*[15]

Ask God to change your heart, fully surrender to Him so that you may become truly rich. In Jeremiah 17, the prophet wrote of this mysterious connection between the heart and finances. Read these words carefully noticing the references to the heart and the associated problems and solutions:

> *Cursed is the man who trusts in man and makes flesh his strength, whose heart turns away from the Lord. He is like a shrub in the desert, and shall not see any good come. He shall dwell in the parched places of the wilderness, in an uninhabited salt land.*
>
> *Blessed is the man who trusts in the Lord, whose trust is the Lord. He is like a tree planted by water, that sends out its roots by the stream, and does not fear when heat comes, for its leaves remain green, and is not anxious in the year of drought, for it does not cease to bear fruit.*
>
> *The heart is deceitful above all things, and desperately sick; who can understand it? I the Lord search the heart and test the mind to give every man according to his ways, according to the fruit of his deeds.*
>
> *Like the partridge that gathers a brood that she did not hatch, so is he who gets riches but not by justice; in the midst of his days they will leave him, and at his end he will be a fool.*[16]

The Lord gets very direct when defining the connection between our heart and our prosperity: A heart that trusts in the world's philosophies is cursed and will be like a shrub in the parched wilderness. In other words, it's toast. But a heart that trusts in God will be like a tree planted by water. It's going to make it through the drought. The comparison is stark and sobering.

When we surrender to God, a transformation of the heart occurs. The former natural man that I labeled the Me Tree becomes a supernatural tree, one I call a He Tree to remind us that it now belongs to Him. And there's our choice: Me Tree or He Tree.

Paul tells us, *"So then, just as you received Christ Jesus as Lord, continue to live in Him, rooted and built up, strengthened in the faith as you were taught, and overflowing with thankfulness."*[17]

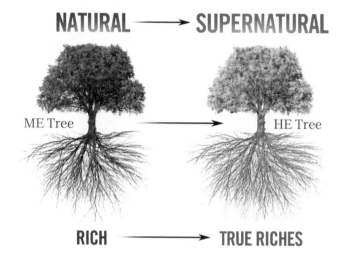

NATURAL ⟶ SUPERNATURAL

ME Tree   HE Tree

RICH ⟶ TRUE RICHES

From the canopy of the He Tree radiates thankfulness for all things in our life, because we have everything to be thankful for, regardless of a poor economy or any temporary circumstance that befalls us. Christians should be the most thankful people in the world because we're filled with the love of the Father and bear His fruit to the desperate world around us.

We all know them when we see them, don't we? We are drawn to those who are not falsely pious or religious or self-righteous but who truly love God with all their heart. They've put aside pretense. They've put aside that yearning to one up somebody else. They've put aside the grabbing for things the world says are important. Free from the striving that once consumed their energy, they now can serve and love other people with joy, without expectation that there's something in it for them.

The Secret of the He Tree

You saw that the Me Tree is controlled by what it loves. So, too, is the He Tree.

We are each controlled by what we love. Love is the most powerful motivator of all and we all want more of what we love.

I want more of God in my tree. I ask Him regularly to feed the roots of my tree so that I can stand strong for Him. The Me Tree is trapped in its own stronghold because it loves the security it sees in money. The He Tree, however, lives in a true fortress built by God Himself because He promises to take care of His own. Which fortress do you prefer? The He Tree's fortress where he does not fear loss, death or destruction, or the prison where the Me Tree lives in continual terror of all three?

Oswald Chambers said, "The remarkable thing about God is that when you fear God, you fear nothing else, whereas if you do not fear God, you will fear everything else."[18]

Compare those two fortresses, one where we live in fear of what we may lose on this earth; the other where we live fearlessly because we know that we can never lose the riches contained within us.

> *Do not be afraid of those who kill the body but cannot kill the soul. Rather, be afraid of the One who can destroy both soul and body in hell.*[19]

In the fortress of the He Tree, our riches are safely stored for eternity where moths, rust and thieves cannot destroy them.

A He Tree and His Widow

You may not know the story of Oswald Chambers. He never spoke to a large group or audience. His ministry lasted only eight years. We might not know of him today were it not for his remarkable wife Gertrude, whom he affectionately called "Biddy."

Biddy was born with a disability; she could not hear well. To compensate, she learned to read lips, and she learned stenography, a shorthand writing method for recording the spoken word. Biddy accompanied her husband on his Bible training missions. Oswald Chambers taught briefly in America and England before moving on to Cairo, Egypt, where he served soldiers fighting in World War I. If you read his words through the eye of someone about to go into battle, you understand the depth and power of Oswald Chambers' teaching. He did not dilute the authority of God's Word.

Oswald Chambers with his Wife Gertrude "Biddy" and Daughter Kathleen

Oswald died at a young age of a ruptured appendix, leaving Biddy and their young daughter alone in Cairo. Biddy was suddenly a single mother in a foreign land where she didn't speak the language. To make matters worse, she didn't have any money, as Oswald had earned only a meager income as a chaplain for the YMCA.

Although it may have appeared outwardly that Oswald's wife and child were poor, Biddy *did* have something. Through the years, she had captured every word that her husband taught from the Bible. No word that he ever spoke fell to the ground because she was present to read his lips, and write them down. After Biddy became a widow, a dear personal friend visiting her in Cairo suggested that she put those words into a devotional. That book would become *My Utmost for His Highest*.

Through God's provision, Biddy and her daughter, Katherine, never had to fear for their financial security again. Since 1927, *My Utmost for His Highest* has become the best-selling devotional ever written. Its sales and popularity continue to this day, over 80 years later. God provided. Oswald, a humble man, who trusted and served God with all of his heart and soul, never had to fear how God would take care of him or his family.[20]

He Trees can live with that kind of fearlessness. We can live with abandonment for God's purposes.

Suffering Loss as a He Tree

> *You sympathized with those in prison and joyfully accepted the confiscation of your property.*[21]

How many people do you know that could do that? "Joyfully accept the confiscation of their property?" In Hebrews, we see the list of many whom I call He Trees because they understood the root of riches. In Hebrews 11:4-38, the passage containing what some call God's Hall of Faith, we see how the beliefs of these saints explain their countercultural reaction to loss: *"you knew that you, yourselves, had better and lasting possessions."*[22]

He Trees can live a great paradox. They are rich but do not fear loss. They are rich but are not self-indulgent. They are rich but live without worry or stress. They are rich in faith even when circumstances are difficult or even horrible. They are rich in treasures to come even though their bank accounts may be empty. He Trees overflow with thankfulness for everything God has lavished on them.

William Borden did not allow the vast wealth he inherited from his rich family to control the direction or purpose of his life. Instead, he decided to serve the Lord and do whatever God called him to do. Contrary to the expectations of family and friends, Borden did not join the family business after college; he followed the Lord's call to serve the least. Borden earned the Phi Beta Kappa award from Yale and graduated from Princeton Seminary with every advantage that the world could offer. He could have followed any path he chose, but Borden was not a Me Tree.

As a He Tree, this remarkable young man carried in his pocket a personal prayer, *"My Lord, enable me to conquer my will and overcome my desires. Not my will but Thine be done."*

Not wanting to be guided by the money he inherited, Borden gave away all of his wealth and put it in a trust to be distributed after his death. And just a little side note about his generosity, William Borden died in 1913, near the same time as J.P. Morgan's death. Both men were Christians, yet, records indicate Borden left far more of his wealth to the cause of Christ than Morgan, one of the wealthiest men on earth at the time.

Like Oswald Chambers, William Borden also died in Cairo at a young age. He was only 25 when he went home to the Lord. After his death, it was dis-

YOUNG MILLIONAIRE RENOUNCES WORLD TO BE MISSIONARY

WILLIAM W. BORDEN

William Whitling Borden makes history, bequeathing $1 million to Christian missions including to China Inland Mission which he was joining, Moody Bible Institute, Moody Church, Princeton

covered that Borden had written in his Bible his innermost thoughts about his experiences. When he gave away his fortune, Borden noted in the front of his Bible, *"No reserves."*

Borden had been in Cairo only a short time before contracting spinal meningitis, which was likely to be terminal. When it looked like he was not going to fulfill the mission he thought God had planned for his life, instead of worrying or fearing death, he again recorded in his Bible, *"No retreat."*

The very last entry in his Bible, probably penned only shortly before his life was over, said, *"No regrets."*[23]

No regrets. Borden was rich in Christ, and there was nothing to fear.

Prayer

Heavenly Father, mere human words cannot do justice to the depth of Your Truth. Lord, I pray for renewed understanding of what it means to be truly rich.

Lord, Scripture reveals the deception of loving only what we can see and feel and touch. I pray that Your Holy Spirit is at work among those who want to be liberated from the control that money has had on their lives.

Heavenly Father, I pray that we become like mighty trees that endure hardship and testing and trials and that our fruit will bless all those around us, in our homes, communities and nations.

Lord, I pray that Your glory will be manifest as we declare that we are rich in Christ, that we do not live with any fear of loss, because what You've given us, Lord, is eternal. We cannot lose our riches in Christ.

Heavenly Father, I thank You. I thank You for the joy it is to be Yours; to be able to say, "You are my stronghold, my protector, my provider. I thank You in Jesus' name. Amen.

DIGGING DEEPER

Chapter 7 – The Root of Riches

Key Points

- He Trees are rich, richer than all Me Trees, regardless of how much money they have accumulated, because the root of riches is found in Christ.

- God makes the He Tree rich in *every way* so that it will give God's riches to others, not hoarding them for itself.

- He Trees can live without fear of loss.

Reflection

[handwritten: redemption, forgiveness, lavish grace, kindness, strength & power of his spirit]

1. Read Romans 11:33; Ephesians 1:7-8, 18; 2:7; 3:8, 16; Philippians 4:19 and Colossians 1:27. List all the ways our true riches in Christ are described.

   [handwritten: fully satisfy every need / Christ in you]

2. Oswald Chambers said, "The remarkable thing about God is that when you fear God, you fear nothing else, whereas if you do not fear God, you will fear everything else."

   How can you apply this insight to your financial circumstances? What would be your answer if someone were to ask, "How rich are you?"

3. What characteristics show that the He Tree is super-natural?

4. Why is fear no longer a controlling factor for a He Tree?

5. God does not expect everyone, like William Borden, to give away all their wealth. However, can you say that you are living your life in such a way as to have "no regrets" by the way you have managed God's money entrusted to you?

6. Complete Non-Negotiable No. 3:

    I must _____ upon and _____
    _____ truth in order to receive
    _____ _____ .

Chapter 7 Endnotes

1. 2 Corinthians 9:11

2. "The World's Billionaires: #1 Carlos Slim Helu & Family," Forbes. com, March 10, 2010 [http://www.forbes.com/lists/2010/10/ billionaires-2010_Carlos-Slim-Helu-family_WYDJ.html]

3. Ephesians 2:7

4. Ephesians 3:8

5. Ephesians 3:16

6. Romans 11:33

7. Ephesians 1:7

8. Ephesians 1:18

9. Philippians 4:19

10. Colossians 1:27

11. Ecclesiastes 12:12

12. Ecclesiastes 12:13-14

13. Ecclesiastes 5:10

14. Proverbs 21:25

15. Proverbs 28:25

16. Jeremiah 17:5-11

17. Colossians 2:6-7

18. *The Bible Exposition Commentary: Old Testament Wisdom and Poetry*, Warren W. Wiersbe, Victor, 2003, Pg. 538

19. Matthew 10:28

20. *Oswald Chambers: Abandoned to God*, David McCasland, Discovery House, 1998

21. Hebrews 10:34

22. Ibid.

23. *Borden of Yale '09*, Mrs. Howard Taylor, Philadelphia China Inland Mission, 1926

CHAPTER EIGHT: INTERLOCKING ROOTS

IT'S BEEN SAID THAT NO MATTER HOW RICH YOU
BECOME OR HOW POWERFUL YOU ARE OR HOW FA-
MOUS YOU BECOME, THAT WHEN YOU DIE, THE SIZE
OF YOUR FUNERAL WILL PROBABLY BE DETERMINED
BY THE WEATHER.

– MICHAEL PRITCHARD

I once attended a funeral where the famous Frank Sinatra song, *I Did It My Way*, was sung as an anthem to celebrate the life of the deceased man. Contrary to their intended purpose, I found the lyrics chilling:

> *And now the end is near*
> *And so I face the final curtain*
> *My friend I'll say it clear*
> *I'll state my case of which I'm certain*
> *I've lived a life that's full*
> *I traveled each and every highway*
> *And more, much more than this*
> *I did it my way . . .*

The song actually celebrates a life of self-exaltation:

> *To think I did all that*
> *And may I say not in a shy way*
> *Oh no, oh no, not me*
> *I did it my way . . .*[1]

I vividly recall how sad the funeral was; all the more so because these self-centered lyrics truly described the way this person had lived his life. I was one of only twelve people attending his funeral service. He did, in fact, do it his way and died a very lonely man because of it. But this is never the case when we do it *God's* way, when we live to please God, instead of ourselves.

As Christians, we live to hear the ultimate affirmation, *"Well done, good and faithful servant."* Those words are recorded in the Parable of the Talents in Matthew 25. While financial in nature, the parable teaches something more than just handling money. It teaches us to be faithful *to God* with money, not to ourselves. God is keeping track of how well we did using the money He provided for His purposes and His Kingdom, not our own. If we fall in love with money, we will seek to be rich in the world's view and miss fulfilling God's purposes for our lives.

We could say that inside every Me Tree there is a He Tree waiting to get out. This understandably causes tension, perhaps even rationalization on the part of the Me Tree who is yet unwilling to be transformed. In fact, some have suggested that I come up with a third kind of tree: a We Tree, if you will. This We Tree tries to serve God *and money.* As I admitted earlier, that was me, trying to be both a Me Tree and a He Tree, thinking the perfect portfolio was a little Jesus and a whole lot of money. And as God said, trying to serve two Masters is impossible.

We must become liberated from the desire for the rewards of men: riches, power and fame. If those are the rewards we seek for our good actions, we have already received payment in full and should expect nothing from the Father. That's as good as it gets.[2]

Recently, I received an e-mail from a missionary working in China who has seen firsthand the persecution of his brothers and sisters in Christ. He's also seen the spiritual battle between the love of money and the love of God. He wrote,

> My second big observation is the grip that economic prosperity has now taken on China. We all hear about government persecution (and it is real), but the silent killer in China

among believers and nonbelievers alike is the idolatry of money.

The best mental picture I can paint to explain this would be America's California Gold Rush of 1849. China is gripped by a gold rush mentality. And this is not limited to non-believers. Now, acknowledging the prosperity we enjoy in America, I do not offer this in judgment of the Chinese people; rather to acknowledge what I believe is a primary tool that Satan is using today in China. Persecution, as history supports, cannot stop the Gospel but the race for economic prosperity can stop the Gospel.

...The silent killer in China...is the idolatry of money.

And when I say economic prosperity, I do not mean earning a living, but rather a desire to be rich. In my observation, this drive is either the number one or number two position in the hierarchy of most Chinese people's priorities, and the result is that it robs time and attention from their pursuit of the Word of God.[3]

A chilling thought, that another forest of Me Trees is rapidly growing in China. This is hardly confined to China. Unfortunately, every nation must deal with this problem.

My friend observed the cancerous nature of the beliefs of the Me Tree, how the love of money penetrates the root system, infecting the tree and constraining the Gospel message. No wonder it's one of Satan's favorite schemes, to enslave us with something that appears to give us liberty.

From my perspective, having traveled around the world numerous times, the love of money is the "number one or number two drive" in people's hearts in *every* nation. As my friend alluded, it's the silent killer of the Church. It's deadly.

Beware of the Bounty on Your Head

I've been inspired by one of our Christian brothers, an evangelical pastor serving in the Middle East. This man is incredibly bold in his nation, publicly proclaiming his faith in Christ despite the risk it poses to his own life. There is reportedly a $65 million bounty on his head. Christians can't put a price on the Gospel, but apparently, it's worth *$65 million* to this man's enemies to stop him from preaching it.[4]

There's something else you should know. There's a bounty on all of our heads. The Enemy has not only taken the Me Trees captive; he wants to have the He Trees taken out, period. There is some amount of money that Satan is offering right now to get you out of the work of fulfilling God's purposes for your life.

There was once such a number hidden in my heart. To my disgrace, in 1999, I was prepared to sell out for $10 million. If I'd been able to achieve that sum of personal net worth, I wouldn't be writing this today. That was the bounty on my head.

By His grace and mercy, God freed me from that idolatry. As I look back on the experience, it's all I can do not to weep in shame. All it would have taken to neutralize my passion for the Gospel was a measly $10 million. Economists like to consider something called the "opportunity cost" of any investment. It's the potential return we give up in order to invest somewhere else. In my view, the "opportunity cost" of attaining that $10 million would have been incalculable.

I came ever so close to being taken out by the bounty on my head because the desire to be wealthy had penetrated my roots. I was defining my success, my significance, my security and my self-worth by the world's standards. The love of money had its ugly roots around my heart, and it was beginning to cause serious tension in my life.

That tension will always exist because we are fighting a battle against the prince of this world. He has placed a bounty on each of our heads. There's a price on your head, some bounty that Satan is offering to distract you from the real riches, a new car, a bigger house, a promotion, inheritance or even a lottery prize, anything to neutralize you, to render you "lukewarm" and useless for God's purposes.

> *I know your deeds, that you are neither cold nor hot. I wish you were either one or the other! So, because you are lukewarm, neither hot nor cold, I am about to spit you out of my mouth. You say, "I am rich; I have acquired wealth and do not need a thing." But you do not realize that you are wretched, pitiful, poor, blind and naked.*[5]

Being lukewarm is putrid to God. The root cause of this offensive condition is the belief that money is a substitute for the riches of Christ. The danger of thinking we are rich and do not need God is the final warning to His Church and to Me Trees everywhere. The hour grows short, but there is still time to become a He Tree:

Being lukewarm is putrid to God. The root cause of this offensive condition is the belief that money is a substitute for the riches of Christ.

> *Those whom I love I rebuke and discipline. So be earnest, and repent. Here I am! I stand at the door and knock. If anyone hears my voice and opens the door, I will come in and eat with him, and he with me. To him who overcomes, I will give the right to sit with me on my throne, just as I overcame and sat down with my Father on his throne. He who has an ear, let him hear what the Spirit says to the churches.*[6]

"Miracle Grow" for the He Tree

The He Tree must have its roots planted deeply in Scripture. It supplies the nutrients to grow good fruit. Sunday sermons give us great teaching, but they are not enough. The He Tree is a Bible reader. You must allow the nutrients of the Living Word to enter your roots so that you grow strong in the faith.

You need this because a He Tree will naturally become a stranger in this world, a strange species, an anomaly. While the He Tree is a towering example of the true riches of Christ, sometimes that will make you a target. Scripture is your shield.

> *Blessed is the man who does not walk in the counsel of the wicked or stand in the way of sinners or sit in the seat of mockers. But his delight is in the law of the Lord, and on his law he meditates day and night.*[7]

God's Word is "Miracle Grow" for the He Tree. It nourishes him and he delights in it.

Several years ago, my teenage son walked in on my devotional time as I was alone in the study. I had just read from my Bible and was thinking how blessed I was to hold God's Word in my hands. Just as I raised the book above my head and kissed the cover, my son walked into the room. He took a quick look at me and said, "Dad, you're weird."

We both laughed at the awkwardness of the moment. Then, with a concerned look, my son asked, "What were you doing?"

I considered just passing over it but decided instead to be transparent with him. I said, "Son, please sit a second and I will explain why I was kissing my Bible."

I took a deep breath and looked him in the eye as I tried to think of a way to express what I felt in my heart. It came out something like this:

"All of my life I've watched people win sporting events. No matter what sport, the winner usually takes the trophy, holds it triumphantly overhead and kisses it as if it's the ultimate reward in life.

"This morning, before you walked in here, I realized that I'm holding the real ultimate reward in my hands. It's better than any silver cup I could ever hold up and kiss."

To know God through His Word is our ultimate reward. To possess the riches that come from loving Him is all we could ever hope to attain.

Blessed is the one . . . whose delight is in the law of the Lord, and who meditates on his law day and night. That person is like a tree planted by streams of water, which yields its fruit in season and whose leaf does not wither, whatever they do prospers.[8]

What a guarantee! What a promise of riches, the true riches. *"Whatever they do prospers."* Allow that to sink into your root system.

The Giant Sequoia

I picked up a Giant Sequoia cone once on a trip to the Sequoia National Forest in California.

I stood in awe as I looked up the trunk of the massive tree pondering the magnificent structure that was once a tiny seed like those contained in the cone I held.

Sequoias can grow to over 300 feet tall, the height of a 30-story building. They are the largest living things on earth, but they originate from a tiny seed the size of an oat flake.

The Giant Sequoia can grow to over 33

Fig. 8.1

Actual size of the cone from the Giant Sequoia tree.

"For as the soil makes the sprout come up and a garden causes seeds to grow, so the Sovereign Lord will make righteousness and praise spring up before all nations" (Isaiah 61:11).

feet in diameter. Twenty average people linking hands would barely circle the base of a mature tree. Their branches can reach seven feet in diameter and their bark has been measured up to 31 inches thick. The oldest recorded Giant Sequoia is estimated to be 3,200 years old.[9]

Scientists aren't sure why the Giant Sequoia lives so long, but I have my own theory. Besides their great size and age, these trees have unusual root systems. Although quite shallow, given the immense size of the trees, their roots seem to interlock with those of other trees around them.

I think these majestic, towering examples of strength and beauty stand firm because beneath the surface their roots are joined together, which gives them the stability they need to endure wind, ice, snow, and even earthquakes! They do not stand alone.

Is that not a beautiful picture of the Body of Christ?

He Trees do not stand alone. With common roots that feed on God's enduring love, they allow their love to flow out and nourish others. He Trees grow to become towering examples of Christ's love and produce the same glorious, priceless fruit wherever they are planted.

When we become He Trees, we join a family. We're the same species of tree as every boy and girl, man and woman, adult or child who has ever entered the kingdom of God. God designed us with interlocking roots that hold us together as a worldwide community. This unique support system eliminates loneliness as we depend upon each other to weather the storms of life.

> *Therefore, since we are surrounded by such a great cloud of witnesses, let us throw off everything that hinders and the sin that so easily entangles. And let us run with perseverance the race marked out for us, fixing our eyes on Jesus, the pioneer and perfecter of faith.*

When I read the opening of Hebrews 12:1-2 (above), I think God is telling us that those just listed in Hebrews 11 (Abel, Enoch, Noah, Abraham, Isaac, Jacob, Joseph, Moses, Rahab,

Samson, David and so many who have gone before us) are all a part of the crowd of witnesses who are watching and cheering for us to run the race marked out for us.

It is like the finishers of the Boston Marathon lining the route as they urge on their fellow participants in an epic race to struggle across the finish line. They urge us to persevere to victory because the victory is not for self-glory but for all who are running for the same prize. Not only are we connected at the root level to all who have been redeemed in the past, but we are also connected to all who will be redeemed after us!

> Man is not a balloon going up into the sky, nor a mole burrowing merely in the earth; but rather a thing like a tree, whose roots are fed from the earth, while its highest branches seem to rise almost to the stars.[10]
>
> – G.K. Chesterton

Rich with Purpose

> Christ's riches are unsearchable, and this doctrine of the gospel is the field this treasure is hidden in.
>
> – Thomas Goodwin

Samuel Marinus Zwemer is one of my heroes. He lived a remarkable life.

At the time of his death in 1952, Zwemer was known as the "Apostle to Islam." He was an American missionary, a scholar and a traveler. Indeed, his travels were so extensive that he was eventually named to the Royal Geographical Society of London.

Zwemer was not out just to collect stickers for his steamer trunk, however. He had determined early in his life that the Muslim world needed the Gospel. This vision drove him to become the first American missionary to the Middle East.

Zwemer was first turned down by the American Missionary Society Board as unqualified. Undaunted in his zeal to bring the Gospel to the Muslim world, he responded, "If a board turns you down from the calling of God, drill a hole in the board and crawl through it anyway."

Zwemer's words grabbed the hearts of many young people of the time. He is credited with influencing more young men and women to go into missionary service than any individual in American history. He fueled the passion of the Student Volunteer Movement. It's been estimated that during the nineteenth century, over 14,000 young people spread out across the world to share the Gospel, some boarding ships with all of their possessions packed inside wooden coffins, believing they would never return.

When Zwemer was turned down for a mission to the Middle East, he made his own way to Bahrain. He and his wife lived there for over 10 years, sharing the Gospel. While there, they were blessed by the birth of two little girls.

Zwemer is known to have made only twelve converts from Islam in his lifetime, but his influence on other missionaries was vast. It seems his roots became quite interlocked.

It was Samuel Zwemer who preached at the funeral of William Borden. He had inspired Borden to give his life to Christ and become a missionary.

Samuel Marinus Zwemer
April 12, 1867 – April 2, 1952

Borden, the wealthy man who could have done anything, chose instead to reap the riches of Christ. Remember his words? *"No reserves. No retreat. No regrets."*

Zwemer also preached at the funeral of Oswald Chambers, and some believe it was Zwemer who encouraged Chambers' widow, Biddy, to collect her late husband's teachings and compile them into a devotional.[11]

Unfazed by the countless disappointments and challenges he faced, Zwemer's roots became interlocked with other giants of the faith, other He Trees, and his influence spread across time and changed the course of history.

The largely unknown Zwemer is my hero for still another reason, however. He lost both of his daughters to dysentery while serving in Bahrain. Many believers, those without their roots deep in the riches of Jesus Christ, would have come home after that tragic loss. Still others might have blamed God Himself, as was suggested to Job when he lost his worldly treasures.

Zwemer remained steadfast in his service to the Lord, however. On the tombstone of those two beloved little girls of Samuel and Amy Zwemer are these words,

Worthy is the Lamb to receive all riches.[12]

Because Zwemer believed that Christ was worthy to receive all, even his two precious children, he was able to press on. He understood the meaning of true riches. Yes, worthy is the Lamb to receive *all* our riches. Anything that you or I will ever claim as our worldly wealth is but a vapor. Compared to our earthly possessions, Christ's true riches are unsearchable.

Think Differently about Money

I don't want to give you the wrong idea that He Trees, those who are truly rich, have to be called to some mission like Borden or Chambers or Zwemer. He Trees serve the Lord in unlimited, creative and effective means of service apart from direct missionary work. One such He Tree I want you to meet is Jay Campbell White.

White did not feel led to the mission field himself. He was a businessman and one with considerable skills. He realized as the Student Volunteer Movement for Foreign Missions began to pick up steam in the late nineteenth century, young missionaries would need a means of support to make their trips abroad. There were far more students willing to go than there were resources to send them. At the time, the foreign mission was still a very new idea in the United States.

The Lord impressed upon White's heart to provide the supplies for all those young people, to help them get into the mission field and established. With clarity of purpose, White spent the rest of his life doing what he called "agitating" the Body of Christ to give more money so the Gospel could go to the ends of the earth.

Do you see the importance of his mission? He was called to "agitate the Body of Christ," to get Christians stimulated to think differently about the use and purpose of money. While his name has not made most people's list of heroes of the faith, White may have done more to spread the Gospel around the world than any other person of his generation.

When his life was nearly over, he wrote, "Nothing can wholly satisfy the life of Christ within His followers except the adaptation of Christ's purposes towards the world."[13]

To "adapt Christ's purposes towards the world" is to serve those He came to redeem for His kingdom, to transform them into His image, from Me Trees into He Trees.

White continued, "Fame, pleasure, and riches are but husks and ashes in contrast with the boundless and abiding joy of working with God for the fulfillment of His eternal plans."[13]

To paraphrase White using my own analogy,

> The Me Tree may become famous, comfortable and rich, but it is not getting anywhere. Its accomplishments are comparable to husks and ashes.
>
> The He Tree, the one who has purposed to fulfill God's eternal plans for his life, will experience something far better than the Me Tree, boundless and abiding joy.

He Trees Are God's Stewards

He Trees, whether entrusted with much or little, become excellent stewards of God's resources because their behavior toward money changes in three key ways:

1. They make money or earn their living with skill by using the gifts and talents that God has given them. By allowing God's unique design for their life to control their career and investment decisions, they experience reduced job stress and, indeed, take great pleasure in their work.

2. They manage the money or resources God entrusted to them with great wisdom. A true steward not only knows God's financial principles, but applies them to every decision. By relying on God's wisdom and not their own, they avoid many of the traps that come from self-reliance. This is not a small distinction between a Me Tree and a He Tree. One sees his financial success as personal business acumen while the other knows his skill is a gift from God that carries responsibility.

3. They use the resources they have to meet their own needs and that of their family while fulfilling God's purposes for their life. How money is spent is another key distinction between the Me Tree and the He Tree; it is not used for personal glory and power, but to bring God glory and spread His goodness.

Restoring the King

Christ must be more than Savior; He must be *Lord* of your life. There's an invisible usurper, a usurper that pushes out the rightful King and sits on the throne of your heart. You must throw out the usurper, the love of money and things. You must make Christ alone Lord of your life.

You are called to be a tree that overcomes the greatest temptations for all mankind: to love self, to love pleasure, and to love money. Answer the call, and be a tree that resists the philosophies of this world and everything in it. Be a tree that loves God with all of your heart, all of your mind and soul. Allow the fruit of your tree to demonstrate to the world that you love the Father, not the world.

You can start by memorizing David's Creed and believing it:

> *Everything in the heavens and earth is yours, O Lord, and this is your kingdom. We adore you as being in control of everything. Riches and honor come from you alone, and you are the Ruler of all mankind; your hand controls power and might, and it is at your discretion that men are made great and given strength.*[14]

Next, redeem all money and possessions for His glory. Take your responsibility as God's steward seriously. He's already given you resources. Now, redeem or repurpose all money and possessions for His glory. Be like Moses, who could have claimed fame and fortune as the son of Pharaoh's daughter, but chose a better reward, a more lasting reward. He suffered to get God's message out to his people.[15]

Be the tree that produces good fruit, the treasures that are unfathomable, unsearchable, and glorious, the true riches of Christ.

Be a tree that embraces your high calling to fulfill His purposes. I implore you to see that the fruit from the He Tree is meant for the benefit of others.

Finally, make daily financial decisions that are based upon God's Truth. In *Managing God's Money*, Randy Alcorn stated his book would not "tell you how to achieve your financial goals, but it will provide the light in which your financial goals should be formulated. That's why the central focus . . . is not insurance but *assurance*, not securities but *security*, not trusts but *trust*, not principal but *principles*, not real estate but *real* estate."[16]

In the next chapter, we'll look at how the Bible guides He Trees to make practical financial decisions.

DIGGING DEEPER

Chapter 8 – Interlocking Roots

Key Points

- The pursuit of worldly riches is a dangerous threat to the church and knowing God's Word is our greatest protection.

- When our roots are transformed, we become a species of tree that is part of God's family for eternity. We are interlocked and interdependent, helping each other to grow and weather the storms of life.

- He Trees are God's stewards equipped to advance His purposes and share His goodness to the ends of the Earth.

Reflection

1. J. Campbell White said, "Fame, pleasure, and riches are but husks and ashes in contrast with the boundless and abiding joy of working with God for the fulfillment of His eternal plans."

   Are your plans aligned with God's plans for your life?

2. Examine the three key changes with money that set He Trees apart from Me Trees. Do you need to change anything about the way you handle money?

3. Read Psalm 1:1-3. Do you see the He Tree in this picture? Are your roots deep in God's Word?

4. Although persecution cannot stop the spread of the Gospel, Chuck believes there is one thing that threatens it. What is it?

5. How would you define the term "idolatry" as it relates to money?

6. In what ways can He Trees provide support for others?

7. If you had to distill it to a single sentence, what is your life purpose?

8. Write out Non-Negotiable No. 3 in the space below:

Chapter 8 Endnotes

1. "My Way," lyrics by Paul Anka

2. See Matthew 6:1

3. For his personal safety, I can't reveal the identity of the missionary in China.

4. While this man has no fear of revealing his identity as a Christian in a Muslim nation, I choose not to aid his enemies in any way by disclosing it here.

5. Revelation 3:15-17

6. Revelation 3:19-21

7. Psalm 1:1-2

8. Psalm 1:1-3

9. *The Giant Sequoia of the Sierra Nevada*, Richard J. Hartesveldt, National Park Service, 1975, Chapter 2. (Online book, http://www. nps.gov/history/history/online_books/science/hartesveldt/chap2.htm)

10. *In His Image*, Dr. Paul Brand and Phillip Yancey, Zondervan Publishing, 1984

11. "The Apostle to Islam: The Legacy of Samuel Zwemer," J. Christy Wilson, Jr., *International Journal of Foreign Missions*

12. Adapted from Revelation 5:11-12

13. J. Campbell White, quoted in *Desiring God: Meditations of a Christian Hedonist*, John Piper, Multnomah, 1986/1996, pg. 188

14. 1 Chronicles 29:11-12 (TLB)

15. See Hebrews 11:24-26

16. *Managing God's Money: A Biblical Guide*, Randy Alcorn, Tyndale, 2011

CHAPTER NINE: FINANCIAL PRACTICES
OF THE HE TREE

ANNUAL INCOME TWENTY POUNDS, ANNUAL
EXPENDITURE NINETEEN AND SIX, RESULT HAPPI-
NESS. ANNUAL INCOME TWENTY POUNDS, ANNUAL
EXPENDITURE TWENTY POUNDS OUGHT AND SIX,
RESULT MISERY.
— CHARLES DICKENS

IT IS POSSIBLE TO LOVE MONEY WITHOUT HAVING IT,
AND IT IS POSSIBLE TO HAVE IT WITHOUT LOVING IT.
— J.C. RYLE

Once we have experienced the supernatural transformation from a Me Tree to a He Tree, we are now rich in every way, regardless of our income! We have the love of God filling our heart, and in return we now share that love with others, generously spreading God's kindness. When our faith is made manifest in our daily behaviors, treasures are stored for us in eternity. According to the promises in Luke 16, those that live in this way will make friends who will welcome them into Heaven.

It is now of great importance to understand the practical advice that God gives to guide the He Trees. Our lives must demonstrate that His ways are far better than man's ways for making and managing money.

He Trees Grow in Rock

To know the truth is only a part of the equation if you want to experience all of God's riches. The other part is to live the truth. We must have the courage to practice what we believe, especially in difficult times. Everyone knows that trees grow rapidly in soft and sandy soil, but the roots have no anchor. When storms come, they are easily toppled and destroyed. However, when the He Tree experiences difficult storms, because he has learned to put God's Words into practice, his roots are deep in the rock of Jesus Christ. He will endure all trials. Jesus used the example of a house to make this promise:

> *Therefore everyone who hears these words of mine and puts them into practice is like a wise man who built his house on the rock. The rain came down, the streams rose, and the winds blew and beat against that house; yet it did not fall, because it had its foundation on the rock. But everyone who hears these words of mine and does not put them into practice is like a foolish man who built his house on sand. The rain came down, the streams rose, and the winds blew and beat against that house, and it fell with a great crash.*[1]

This parable illustrates that storms are not optional for either the foolish Me Tree or the wise He Tree. Both are battered by the same storms, trials and tests. One, however, is prepared for stormy weather, the one that has acted upon God's Truth.

The Bible is full of practical advice to prepare us for the financial challenges that we all must face. Those that are wise will follow these practices. My list is not exhaustive, but it is the essence of what is necessary for the He Tree to overcome every financial problem.

Work Hard at All Times

> *Work gives meaning to life. It is the form in which we make ourselves useful to others.*[2]

This quote, by Lester DeKoster, the former director of the Calvin College and Seminary library, condenses the importance of this simple yet profound truth, that work is the basis for all that we are put on earth to accomplish.

You and I were designed by God to work. Work is not a curse that we must endure, it is the way we experience purpose, meaning and joy. It's what we were created to do . . . work and *produce*. In fact, *not* working takes a greater toll on us in the long run. I don't mean resting and taking care of our bodies, but avoiding work *altogether*, which is the road to misery and ruin.

Chuck Colson, founder of Prison Fellowship, wrote, "God created human beings in His own image and part of being 'in His image' means that we are workers—like God Himself. That's where that innate, inner drive for work comes from. Work is part of God's nature."[3]

Since we are created in God's image and divinely ordained for work, we are to rule over the lower creation. This distinctive trait allows for self-expression, the potential to be used for great causes to serve the needs of the world and to bring glory to God in the process.

As He Trees, our work should be excellent in every way. Christians should be the most desired of all employees or employers in the world. Why? Because we believe in the dignity of hard work and strive to do our best with the motivation that we are representing the God who created us for His purposes. His Word gives us clear instruction to work hard:

Whatever your hands find to do, do it with all your might.[4]

You shall work six days.[5]

If anyone will not work, neither let him eat.[6]

In my travels, I've experienced cultures where work is not valued or practiced among the men in the community. The consequences that result from these practices are always misery, suffering and extreme poverty. Far too often, Christians attempt to treat only the symptoms of poverty through generosity and charitable help alone. Unfortunately, if we avoid dealing with the root issue in these cultures, a lack of knowledge of God and His teachings, their errant beliefs remain unchanged. Misery simply returns when the giving stops.

However, if we make it our mission to plant He Trees in this community, the bountiful fruit produced by transformed people will be an ongoing witness to the goodness of God and His ways. But that's not all!

Lester DeKoster expanded his insight into the exponential impact of our work on the whole of civilization:

> Lay a blanket of seeds upon a field, and behold, a harvest! Lay a blanket of work upon the world, and behold, a civilization![7]

Work in the Area Where God Has Given You Skill

It honors the Father when we are true to work according to our design. Ralph Mattson and Arthur Miller make this point quite well in their book, *Finding a Job You Can Love:*

> We please God when we act the way we are designed to act, when we are who God designed us to be. When such actions are carried out with the intention of being expressions of love to Him, they do in fact become expressions of love to Him.[8]

A friend once helped me understand the importance of knowing God's unique design of my inner man. He encouraged me to seek understanding of my gifts, interests, skills and values and to operate accordingly in my chosen area of work. He said, "Chuck, a John Deere Tractor is not a Mercedes Benz and a Bulldog is not a Chihuahua, so you would not attempt to plow a field driving a Mercedes or train the Bulldog to sit in your lap. Likewise you should not work in an area where God has not designed you to be successful." How true.

Can you imagine a bluebird trying to be a woodpecker just so it can attract more attention? His bill is not equipped for drilling holes. A bluebird honors its Creator by being a very beautiful bluebird. Likewise, those who recognize their talents and use them for the glory of God become a magnificent testimony to the work of the Creator.

Since our work is meant to reflect God's glory, we need to recognize this as the proper motivation for our labors. Our work is a sacred act of worship. It is a daily opportunity to share God's goodness. If we are motivated by greed, pride or a desire to become powerful in man's world, we fail to achieve our life's purpose.

> So whether you eat or drink or whatever you do, do it all for the glory of God.[9]

> For we are God's workmanship, created in Christ Jesus to do good works, which God prepared in advance for us to do.[10]

> . . . And every skilled person to whom the Lord has given skill and ability to know how to carry out all the work of constructing the sanctuary are to do the work just as the Lord has commanded.[11]

Eliminate All Debt

A He Tree should be free of all masters except Jesus Christ. Debt puts one in the position of slave to the lender. Jesus Christ was a slave, but only to the will of His Father; he had no human masters. We should be free to completely obey God's will at any time.

> Owe no one anything, except to love each other, for the one who loves another has fulfilled the law.[12]

> Just as the rich rule over the poor, so the borrower is servant to the lender.[13]

Here are the steps you can follow to get completely out of debt:

1. **Stop any form of borrowing.** This includes credit cards and loans from family and friends. Consumer credit is our most common source of indebtedness, and the sooner you stop borrowing, the sooner you will get out of debt.

2. **Develop a spending plan.** A spending plan gives you the freedom to spend money with a purpose or strategy. It simplifies daily decisions and ensures that your priorities will be met. The deeper in debt you are, the more restrictive your spending plan will need to be while you pay down debt.

3. **Work out a payback plan with your creditors.** Most creditors are willing to work with people who honestly want to repay them.

4. **Learn to trust God and you will experience self-control.** That sounds like a paradox, but it's the key to getting out of debt and staying out of debt. The more you trust God, the less you'll want to borrow.

5. **Break the hold materialism has on your heart through giving.** The cure for wanting things is generosity. Begin giving ten percent of your income to support God's work to demonstrate He is the highest priority in your life.

6. **Seek counsel and advice.** Pray and ask God to place others in your life that will gladly share their wisdom and experience to help you achieve your goals.

Take Care of Your Family

If anyone does not provide for his own, and especially for those of his household, he has denied the faith and it worse than an unbeliever.[14]

God's financial plan is balanced. He has given us the primary responsibility of caring for our own flesh and blood. While we are to make giving and sharing the ultimate goal of our lives, we should use the rewards of our labor or work to first ensure that our family needs are met. However, be careful not to become addicted to an ever-increasing lifestyle of comfort.

John Piper wrote, "The issue is not how much a person makes. Big industry and big salaries are a fact of our times, and they are not necessarily evil. The evil is in being deceived into thinking a $100,000 salary must be accompanied by a $100,000 lifestyle. God has made us to be conduits of His grace. The danger is in thinking the conduit should be lined with gold. It shouldn't. Copper will do."[15]

When you follow God's principles for work, diligence and excellence in all you do, rewards are sure to follow. Be careful to avoid feeling guilty when you experience an increase in your income or assets. View this as God entrusting you with greater responsibility as His steward. Use your increase to give more glory to Him.

Help Others Prosper

The emphasis of the false "health, wealth and prosperity gospel" is on personal enrichment. Not only is that message unsupported by Scripture, it's exactly backwards!

Imagine if you are bucket. The prosperity gospel teaches that we can claim or demand of God to fill our bucket with money and possessions almost as a magical act that will occur without any responsibility or expectation on our part other than "sowing a seed of faith." This is an attempt to manipulate God to get what we want.

A more accurate understanding is that we are funnels and God wants to pour into those funnels so that we can bless others. God's message of prosperity in the Bible is that we are to be His conduits to help others prosper. That is, to discover their riches in Christ.

God's Part, Our Part

> *"For I know the plans I have for you," declares the Lord, "plans to prosper you and not to harm you, plans to give you hope and a future."*[16]

This verse should cause all of our hearts to leap with joy regardless of our current circumstances. It was delivered to God's people who were held captive in Babylon. They lived in something akin to a modern day refugee camp.

The Israelites had nothing when He spoke these comforting words to them. We take much hope and comfort from these words today, but we tend to skip over the Lord's instructions given just a few verses earlier. God had His part, but the Jews had theirs:

> *Also, seek the peace and prosperity of the city to which I have carried you into exile. Pray to the Lord for it, because if it prospers, you too will prosper.*[17]

The Jews were to pray for and seek to help their enemies prosper, the very people who were holding them prisoner. In fact, the Lord said that their own prosperity *depended* on their willingness to help the Babylonians prosper! I call this the Principle of Reciprocal Prosperity. It is one of the most misunderstand financial truths in the Bible.

What are we to take from this? The Lord wanted to make Himself known to the Babylonians through funnels, not buckets. He had placed His people inside this foreign land to share His goodness.

If you are a businessperson, you will no doubt see the wisdom of the Principle of Reciprocal Prosperity. All successful businesses have a win-win attitude and strategy. If the company is able to serve others and meet the needs of the customer, the business will also grow and prosper. If it does not meet those needs, it will cease to exist. It's the very same principle here. A He Tree is placed by God where the fruit of that tree can be shared so others will have their needs met and the blessings of

God will be spread. If we help others achieve their goals, we too will be able to achieve ours. This is the aspect of serving others above ourselves that guides a good businessman or woman.

Save a Portion of All Your Earnings

We must take care when saving money because it can be either good or evil, depending on the motive.

On the one hand, it's wise to save money for the future:

> The wise man saves for the future, but the foolish man spends whatever he gets.[18]

On the other hand, the Bible makes it clear we are not to rely on money as a substitute for our dependence on God.

> Yes, a person is a fool to store up earthly wealth but not have a rich relationship with God.[19]

The practice of saving money varies widely by culture. I have been in African villages where saving money is nonexistent. Instead of money, these villagers view their relationships with family and neighbors as a form of savings and protection against future needs. While we might be tempted to judge them harshly for not saving, we are advised to respect the poor for being "rich in faith." Often, they have no other options but to trust God for their daily bread.

I have also taught in Asian cities where the average personal saving rate is 30% or more of their annual income. They have a high degree of discipline and control that enables them to store for the future. Often this drive is from what they describe as a "survival instinct."

Does the one culture practice wasteful spending and the other hoarding? We should be careful not to condemn or endorse either group without knowing their true motive for saving or not saving money.

Wasteful spending presumes that God will always provide for us even if we fail to do our part. Hoarding, on the other hand, presumes that we are "on our own" and that God will not keep His promise to provide for our needs. Both must be avoided.

We must have financial surplus to meet unplanned expenses and to share with others in need. However, it's also important to avoid growing dependent on money alone. Perceived financial "independence" can in reality be a hidden form of financial dependence, relying on money instead of God. Hebrews 13:5 should govern our attitude about financial surplus, regardless of the amount we save.

> *Keep your lives free from the love of money and be content with what you have, because God has said, "Never will I leave you; never will I forsake you."*

The implication here is that money will leave you and forsake you. God is making it known that money alone as a form of security is unreliable and that we are to trust Him to provide.

Never Compromise Your Integrity

Your integrity is priceless. It's interesting that integrity is highly prized in the world's view, as well as God's.

Integrity comes from the root word *integer*, meaning whole or complete. A person with integrity is whole, complete, not made less by dishonesty. This is a true description of the person who is genuine or authentic.

The Bible summarizes the life of the kings of Israel and Judea with a single measurement. Either the king did what was right in the eyes of God, or he did evil. The entire life's work of a king boiled down to that one measurement: integrity before God. In the same way, our lives will be measured by our integrity and any small deviation can destroy it.

During a talk I gave to about 200 business people in China, I was asked how the Christian businessman could operate in a system that was controlled by corrupt practices. White-collar fraud and bribery are rampant there, as is the case in many parts of the world.

I immediately thought of Joseph and Daniel who were both men of absolute integrity operating in hostile, corrupt nations. I replied, "If you are willing to pay the price of short-term losses, even if it means becoming the last honest man in China, you will eventually be recognized for your integrity. Even a corrupt ruler wants an honest man to run his affairs. Joseph went to prison and Daniel went to the lions' den for their integrity, but both were exalted to the highest levels of responsibility in their corrupt nations."

I then read from Isaiah 33:15-16:

> *He who walks righteously and speaks what is right, who rejects gain from extortion and keeps his hand from accepting bribes, who stops his ears against plots of murder and shuts his eyes against contemplating evil, this is the man who will dwell on the heights, whose refuge will be the mountain fortress. His bread will be supplied, and water will not fail him.*

The room was filled with spontaneous applause, not for my response, but for the wisdom and hope shared from God's Word.

God's promises to the righteous man are staggering, and His warnings to the evil are terrifying. To be truly rich, we must conduct every area of our lives with absolute integrity.

> *The house of the righteous contains great treasure, but the income of the wicked brings them trouble.*[20]

> *He who profits illicitly troubles his own house, but he who hates bribes will live.*[21]

Use All Resources to Advance God's Kingdom

The Bible never condemns wealth; it only warns or condemns when money is gained by doing evil or used for foolish purposes.

Like any organization, Crown Financial Ministries looks for honest men to serve in our missions around the world. It hasn't always been easy to find them. Eventually, our continent leader in Africa developed a method to determine who should join our organization. He calls it the "Money Test" and it works like this.

When someone expresses interest in joining Crown's mission, the leader arranges a phone call and asks the candidate to submit a budget for launching the ministry in the candidate's country.

After reviewing the budget, the leader will say that he wants to fly out to meet in person for an interview and that he is sending a few hundred dollars in advance for expenses. He asks the candidate to keep receipts for how the money is used.

Later, after the face-to-face interview is completed, the leader asks for the receipts. In almost every case, receipts are produced showing the money was spent on hotel rooms, meals and other expenses related to the visit. The interview concludes.

Unbeknownst to the candidate, the leader then stays an extra day in that country contacting hotels, restaurants and car rental companies to ask about their rates. All too often, the receipts indicate costs higher than the actual rates, indicating they've been falsified and the difference was pocketed by the prospective new hire.

Candidates who fail this small "Money Test" lose their opportunity for the far greater reward of a long-term job.

I believe God gives each one of us a "Money Test." He advances resources to us and will demand an accounting of how we spend the money. He is only interested in one question: Did you use money for your own interests or His?

> So if you have not been trustworthy in handling worldly wealth, who will trust you with true riches?[22]

To those who pass the "Money Test," the long- term rewards are defined as the true riches. These are the blessings of living according to God's financial principles and enjoying both the present and eternal rewards for faithfulness to Him. These are the riches that cannot be lost, stolen or destroyed in contrast to mere worldly wealth.

> The blessing of the Lord makes rich, and He adds no sorrow with it.[23]

Make Generosity the Focus of Your Life

God wants to spare us the sorrow that can accompany worldly wealth. He does that by asking us to trust Him enough to give part of it away. He wants us to let go of it.

God took a risk to bless us so richly. The risk is that we might fall in love with the *blessings* and forget the One who blessed. To minimize that risk, God designed an economy quite apart from the world. It's based on sharing, not hoarding or squandering. It is vital that we learn to be generous with others to avoid the dangers of trusting in our possessions. As we advance God's kingdom by practical means, we experience true riches through giving.

We must stop putting our security in the abundance that God has given us.

> *In everything I did, I showed you that by this kind of hard work we must help the weak, remembering the words the Lord Jesus himself said: "It is more blessed to give than to receive."*[24]

> *Honor the Lord with your wealth, with the firstfruits of all your crops.*[25]

Be the He Tree

Your heart has been changed, your roots transformed and your mind renewed by God's Truth. You are now ready to put principles into action. You must move from one who *knows* to one who *does*. When you step out in faith, taking action based on truth, you become a He Tree.

This is God's great desire for you. He wants you to be the tree that gives shelter to those who are hurting, who are weak and who are in need of the shade and the delicious, refreshing fruit that comes from your branches.

Be the tree that understands true riches are found in Him, Jesus Christ, alone.

DIGGING DEEPER

Chapter 9 – Financial Practices of the He Tree

Key Points

- Our financial house will be built upon sand or rock. Both will get tested but only one will endure the storms.

- The financial practices of the He Tree set it apart from the Me Tree and enable it to be used for God's purposes.

- God wants to us to put His truth into action.

Reflection

1. John Piper wrote, "The issue is not how much a person makes. Big industry and big salaries are a fact of our times, and they are not necessarily evil. The evil is in being deceived into thinking a $100,000 salary must be accompanied by a $100,000 lifestyle. God has made us to be conduits of His grace. The danger is in thinking the conduit should be lined with gold. It shouldn't. Copper will do."

   What adjustments, if any, do you need to make your lifestyle? Are you living a golden lifestyle on a copper income?

2. Read Jeremiah 29:4-13. How does the Principle of Reciprocal Prosperity apply to your current job, your business or your approach to serving others?

3. Which of these key financial practices do you need the most help to improve?

   ☐ Working hard at all times

   ☐ Working in an area where God has gifted you

   ☐ Eliminating all debt

   ☐ Taking care of your family with an appropriate lifestyle

   ☐ Helping others prosper

   ☐ Saving a portion of all your earnings

   ☐ Guarding your integrity

   ☐ Using all resources to advance God's kingdom

   ☐ Making generosity the focus of your life

4. Why is it so important not only to hear God's Word, but also to apply it?

5. Name some consequences that result in cultures where work is not valued.

6. How can your work or occupation reflect God's glory?

7. Explain what it means to be a "funnel" instead of a "bucket."

8. What is the difference between saving and hoarding?

9. Repeat from memory Non-Negotiable No. 3.

Chapter 9 Endnotes

1. Matthew 7:24-27
2. *Work: The meaning of Your Life—A Christian Perspective*, Lester DeKoster, Christians Liberty Press, 2010, pg. 9
3. Op. cit., Chuck Colson, quoted in DeKoster
4. Ecclesiastes 9:10
5. Exodus 34:21
6. 2 Thessalonians 3:10
7. Op. cit., DeKoster
8. *Finding a Job You Can Love*, Ralph Mattson, Arthur Miller, Thomas Nelson, 1982
9. 1 Corinthians 10:31
10. Ephesians 2:10
11. Exodus 36:1
12. Romans 13:8 (ESV)
13. Proverbs 22:7 (NLT)
14. 1 Timothy 5:8
15. *Desiring God: Meditations of a Christian Hedonist*, John Piper, Multnomah, 2011
16. Jeremiah 29:11
17. Jeremiah 29:7
18. Proverbs 21:20 (TLB)
19. Luke 12:21 (NLT)
20. Proverbs 15:6
21. Proverbs 15:27 (NASB)
22. Luke 16:11
23. Proverbs 10:22 (ESV)
24. Acts 20:35
25. Proverbs 3:9

CHAPTER TEN: OUR TREE OF LIFE

FOR WHAT DOES IT PROFIT A MAN TO GAIN THE
WHOLE WORLD, AND FORFEIT HIS SOUL?[1]

In 1886, Vicksburg, Mississippi candy store owner, Joseph A. Biedenharn, began experiencing brisk sales of a new fountain beverage priced at five cents a glass. The formula for the drink was actually created by another man, John S. Pemberton.

Over the next several years, the popularity of the fountain drink grew exponentially. In 1892, Pemberton sold the formula and patents to Asa Candler, an Atlanta businessman.

Candler formed a company around the drink and expanded its promotion and sales across the country. In 1895, he reported to shareholders that the beverage was sold and drunk in every state and territory in the United States.

Despite its popularity, however, the drink was still only available as a fountain beverage. Then, in 1899, Chattanooga, Tennessee attorneys Benjamin F. Thomas and Joseph B. Whitehead convinced Candler to sell them the rights to put the beverage in bottles and sell it across most of the United States—all for the unbelievable sum of $1.[2]

The product, which by now I'm sure you've guessed is Coca-Cola,° took off from there and became one of the most recognized brands in the world.

There's one more twist to the story, however. In 2010, the Coca-Cola Company bought back those bottling rights in a deal reportedly worth $12.3 billion![3]

Some would call the original purchase by Thomas and Whitehead one of the greatest business deals of all time. As spectacular as the Coca-Cola story became, it does not compare to the negotiation that took place between Satan and Jesus for our purchase.

The Greatest Negotiation of All Time

When Jesus had fasted for 40 days and 40 nights in the wilderness and was physically weakened by hunger, Satan sensed an opportunity to derail the course of human history. The evil one attempted to negotiate a deal with Jesus and he went for the total win. He tempts Christ with the largest deal ever put on the table in a true winner-take-all offer.

Sitting atop a very high mountain with a panoramic view of the kingdoms and riches of the world, Satan makes an offer he's sure Christ can't refuse. I envision the evil one standing with arms extended, palms turned towards the sky like a game show host displaying shiny prizes to contestants . . .

"All this I will give you," he said, *"if you will bow down and worship me."*[4]

I can hear the sinister, echoing voice of Satan, the Great Carnival Barker . . .

"Step right up! Win the grand prize!"

It seems almost laughable that Satan, in his blind arrogance, would expect the Son of God to fall for that one. We easily see through the ruse. What we often miss, however, is that an equally poor trade is offered to each one of us every single day of our lives.

"Look, you can have this if you will only _____ ."

Fill in the blank with any of the countless ways we are deceived by Satan. It is his constant ploy to entice us to exchange material things, riches, power and pleasure for submission to his ways. He seeks to buy us all in exchange for trinkets.

Putting Belief into Action

In Matthew 4, Jesus showed us how to be the He Tree. The Father sent Him into the world to teach us how to apply His Truth to our lives.

Satan tempted Jesus with three philosophies of this world to see if they could control Him. All three are philosophies that control the Me Tree. Allow me to paraphrase the evil one:

"Feed yourself! You can do it! Use that godly power for yourself. Behave like I want you to behave!" But Jesus would not take the bait.

"Jump! Impress people with your power!" But Jesus didn't budge.

Finally, Satan said, *"Look around and everything that you see can be yours. Avoid going to the cross. Avoid being mocked and put to shame. Bypass the injustice and humiliation! Just worship me and this vast beautiful world can all be yours, now! You can be rich, now!"* But Jesus stood firm.

This is the most pivotal negotiation in the history of the world. Satan was seeking a compromise with the Savior to derail Him from going to the cross. Without Christ's ultimate sacrifice, there would be no redemption. Satan sought to prevent God from demonstrating His incredible mercy and love for a lost world. Jesus would have none of it, and resisted Satan's guile by powerfully stating what he *believed.*

"Turn the stones to bread!"

"No, Man does not live by bread alone."

Man does not live by bread, or money or possessions alone. Yes, we need bread, but we must also live by the Word of God. Money alone is not sufficient; we must live with our roots in the Word of God.

Satan mocked Him for not jumping from the pinnacle of the temple.

> *"The angels will catch you anyway . . . just do it!"*
>
> *"No. We're not to put the Lord, our God, to the test."*

He Trees do not take foolish risks and then say, "God, I'm jumping now so catch me."

In my years of working to help Christians solve their financial problems, I've often heard people say, "I'm in a financial bind . . . I jumped into this deal . . . I jumped into this purchase . . . I jumped into this house . . . I jumped into this refinance. . . ." They jumped and expected God to catch them!

He Trees do not live that way. He Trees learn to wait on the Lord. They have faith in Him and the resulting fruit is patience and self-control. Their beliefs prevent them from jumping when the evil one tempts. They know they are not alone in the battle.

> *He Trees learn to wait on the Lord.*

Jesus walked away from the negotiating table. He turned down the short cut to worldly fame and fortune because His roots held firm. Not for a second did He consider Satan's preposterous deal.

> *Away from me, Satan! For it is written: "Worship the Lord your God, and serve him only."* [5]

The course of history was changed when Adam and Eve fell under the lies of the evil one. History was again changed when Jesus withstood Satan's temptation in the wilderness.

Instead of avoiding the cross (and becoming a Me Tree), Christ ultimately paid the price and claimed something far more valuable than the kingdoms of this world. He redeemed His people from a world stained by sin and death and assured our place in the marvelous Kingdom of God.

Scripture marks the end of this dramatic confrontation in the wilderness with these words:

> *Then the devil left him, and angels came and attended him.*[6]

What a beautiful expression of the concern our Heavenly Father has for the He Tree who stands firm. Expect God's blessing when you walk away from Satan's table.

Jesus showed us how to walk away, how to resist the world's temptations. He is our *supernatural* Tree of Life. I thank God that Jesus loved us and wanted us, in spite of our sin and rebellion, more than He wanted worldly riches and power.

He Wants to Change Our Hearts

One of the most powerful macro-economic promises in Scripture is found in Ezekiel 36. Those who preach the false prosperity gospel, however, focus on only part of the passage, God's promise of provision, as though we could call down God's blessing like a bank calls in a loan.

It just doesn't work like that. A transformation must take place before any expectation of a blessing.

> *For I will take you out of the nations; I will gather you from all the countries and bring you back into your own land.*
>
> *I will sprinkle clean water on you, and you will be clean; I will cleanse you from all your impurities and from all your idols.*
>
> *I will give you a new heart and put a new spirit in you; I will remove from you your heart of stone and give you a heart of flesh.*
>
> *And I will put my Spirit in you and move you to follow my decrees and be careful to keep my laws.*
>
> *You will live in the land I gave your forefathers; you will be my people, and I will be your God. I will save you from all your uncleanness.*[7]

The Sovereign, All-Powerful God of the Universe makes it clear that a complete and radical transformation of the heart is not only possible, it's mandatory and *He* will do it.

This is the promise available to every Me Tree. Let yourself be transformed, become a He Tree, and as a nation of He Trees, all will know and share His blessing:

> *I will call for the grain and make it plentiful and will not bring famine upon you.*
> *I will increase the fruit of the trees and the crops of the field, so that you will no longer suffer disgrace among the nations because of famine.*
> *Then you will remember your evil ways and wicked deeds, and you will loathe yourselves for your sins and detestable practices.*[8]

To the He Trees, those whose roots have been transformed and have love for the Father coursing through them, who live by His laws, using money for His purposes, God promises to bring macroeconomic blessing and to remove the disgrace of famine.

Some argue that this promise was made only to ancient Israel, which it certainly was; but how then do we explain the abundance God has showered on the United States, a country founded on Judeo-Christian principles, with a strong heritage of faith? How do we explain the spiritual and financial contrast between North and South Korea?

How then do you begin the transformation of your roots, turning your heart from stone to flesh? By embracing the good news that Jesus Christ came to give you His life.

Jesus Is the Tree of Life

> *A shoot will come up from the stump of Jesse; from his roots a Branch will bear fruit.*[9]

> *In that day the Root of Jesse will stand as a banner for the peoples; the nations will rally to him, and his place of rest will be glorious.*[10]

As He Trees, our roots interlock with the roots of Jesus. The strength we gain from our relationship with Christ allows us to bear good fruit.

In Ezekiel 47, the prophet uses the image of water to describe this relationship. He has a vision of a trickle of water flowing out of the Temple of God. The water rises from ankle deep to knee deep to waist deep and higher, eventually becoming a beautiful river of fresh water, too deep to cross, giving life wherever it flows. Is it any surprise what we find drawing life from God's refreshing waters? Trees!

> *Fruit trees of all kinds will grow on both banks of the river. Their leaves will not wither, nor will their fruit fail. Every month they will bear fruit, because the water from the sanctuary flows to them. Their fruit will serve for food and their leaves for healing.*[11]

Again, we are compared to trees, eternal trees that will bear good fruit year round. Not just one season a year, *but every month without end*. As He Trees, our fruit will serve for food and our leaves for healing others. We are only able to do this because our roots have been transformed, and instead of feeding on the world's false promises, they draw in the Living Water of Jesus Christ.

In Genesis 2, we learned of the tree of the knowledge of good and evil. We dwell on this tree of death because it was instrumental in the fall of Adam and Eve. We often overlook the other tree growing in the Garden of Eden, the tree of life.

The tree of life shows up again in the very last chapter of Scripture, Revelation 22, where John has nearly the same vision as Ezekiel:

> *Then the angel showed me the river of the water of life, as clear as crystal, flowing from the throne of God and of the Lamb down the middle of the great street of the city. On each side of the river stood the tree of life, bearing twelve crops of fruit, yielding its fruit every month. And the leaves of the tree are for the healing of the nations.*[12]

Now, in the final chapter, it is revealed that Christ is the Tree of Life, and that He has been with us since the very beginning in the garden. Jesus Christ laid down His life on the Cross, a tree of death, to validate for all time that He is in fact the Tree of Life. When we receive His life in us, we become His. He wants us to join together with Him and interlock our roots with His!

Through His life, Jesus demonstrated for you and me how to be a He Tree. He showed us the way. He showed us the eternal purposes of God.

We arrive now at another paradox. The wisest, most *practical* thing you can do is apply *spiritual* truth to your life. Only spiritual truth will transform your understanding of riches and allow you to escape the philosophies of this world.

> *The most practical thing that you can do is to believe God's Word and allow your roots to interlock with the roots of the Tree of Life.*

The most practical thing that you can do is to believe God's Word and allow your roots to interlock with the roots of the Tree of Life. Only He Trees, those who have offered themselves as living sacrifices to do God's perfect will line the river flowing from the Temple and join together to become the forest that God designed for His kingdom and glory.

You and I are called to be He Trees so that the priceless fruit of God will burst forth and bring the true riches to the world. We are called to bear this fruit, the Gospel, to others throughout the world and bring healing to the nations.

Only the Spirit of God can transform you from a Me Tree into a He Tree. You can't fake it. You can't manufacture it with humanism. You can't demand it as payment for your good behavior. Only God can make a He Tree.

I beg you now to ask Him to make you a He Tree. Ask Him to transform your roots so they will seek only His riches, not the world's false promises of wealth. He wants to do it. He is only waiting for you to ask.

> I am Thy servant to do Thy will, and that will is sweeter to me than position or riches or fame, and I choose it above all things on Earth or in Heaven.[13]

Prayer

Heavenly Father, we thank You for the revelation of Your Word. We are so grateful that You cared enough to tell us exactly what to avoid, the love of money that will kill us, that will make us lukewarm, insignificant and unproductive.

Lord, we thank You for allowing people like us, with flawed roots, to be called Your people, to have our names added to those You love.

We thank You for calling us to do Your will, for allowing us to bear Your healing fruit to the nations; to bring glory to Your kingdom.

Lord, we seek not fame or fortune or power or the esteem of men, but only to reflect Your glory. For we no longer love those things, Lord. We love only You.

We give these thanks in the name of Christ alone, the Tree of Life, who gave His life to redeem ours. Amen.

DIGGING DEEPER

Chapter 10 – Our He Tree

Key Points

- Satan tempted Jesus with promises to make Him a Me Tree, but Christ rejected every offer. Jesus applied spiritual truth to counter the evil one's lies.

- Jesus wants you to love Him with all of your heart, mind and body.

- He is the Tree of Life, and we will be transformed into His image to bring healing to the nations.

Reflection

1. Has the Great Carnival Barker, Satan, tempted you with a negotiation to distract you from fulfilling God's purposes for your life?

2. Read Matthew 4:1-11. Note the ways Jesus uses Non-Negotiable No. 3 to counter the attacks of Satan.

   One lives by God's words
   Serve & worship God only

3. Read Genesis 2:9, 3:24 and Revelation 22:1-2. To what
    is Jesus compared? Describe the fruit we will bear after
    we are transformed into His likeness.

    a diff. kind each mo
    good for food
    pleasing to eye
    life

4. Write out the three Non-Negotiables from memory.

    No. 1: I agree _____

    _____

    _____

    _____ .

    No. 2: I must _____

    _____

    _____

    _____ .

    No. 3: I must _____

    _____

    _____

    _____ .

5. What strategy did Jesus use to resist the temptations of
    Satan?

6.   Read Ezekiel 36:24-29. How is the transformation from
     a "heart of stone" to a "heart of flesh" accomplished?

     cleansing
     holy spirit

7.   What, if anything, is preventing you from becoming a
     He Tree?

8.   Has your definition of "rich" changed? If so, how?

9.   Read and consider John 13:17.

     the obedient
     are blessed

10. Now go on to read and complete the 12 Practical Appli-
     cations on the following pages.

Chapter 10 Endnotes

1. Mark 8:36 (NASB)

2. "125 Years of Sharing Happiness, A Short History of the Coca-Cola Company," Coca-Cola Company booklet, 2011 [http://www.thecoca-colacompany.com/heritage/pdf/Coca-Cola_125_years_booklet.pdf]

3. "Coca-Cola to Purchase Bottler in $12.3 Billion Deal," Bloomberg, February 25, 2010 [http://www.bloomberg.com/apps/news?pid=newsarchive&sid=ayIm0dQClBNA]

4. Matthew 4:9

5. Matthew 4:10

6. Matthew 4:11

7. Ezekiel 36:24-29

8. Ezekiel 36:29-31

9. Isaiah 11:1

10. Isaiah 11:10

11. Ezekiel 47:12

12. Revelation 22:1-2

13. *The Pursuit of God*, A.W. Tozer, Tribeca Books, 2011

THE ROOT OF RICHES
12 PRACTICAL APPLICATIONS

I now commit to take the following actions:

1. I will read the entire Bible seeking to know the Author, not just the content or the principles. I will allow God's truth to sink into my heart, transform my mind and change my behavior.

2. I will earn my living by using the skills and talents that God has given me. I will rely upon God's unique design for my life to control my career and investment decisions.

3. I will manage the money and resources God entrusted to me with great care by learning and applying His financial principles to every decision.

4. I will use the resources I've been given to meet my needs and that of my family while seeking to fulfill God's purposes for my life. I will avoid personal glory, choosing instead to bring glory to God and to spread His goodness to others.

5. I will memorize David's Creed from 1 Chronicles 29:11-12 (TLB):

   Everything in the heavens and earth is yours, O Lord, and this is your kingdom. We adore you as being in control of everything. Riches and honor come from you alone, and you are the Ruler of all mankind; your hand controls power and might, and it is at your discretion that men are made great and given strength.

6. I will work hard at all times knowing that by being productive and useful to others, my needs will be supplied and I will bring glory to God.

7. I will stop borrowing money and begin working to eliminate all past and current debt. My only outstanding obligation will be the debt to love others.

8. I will reduce my lifestyle expenses in order to increase my financial capacity to serve God.

9. I will apply the Principle of Reciprocal Prosperity by seeking first to help others prosper. By serving them and seeking their well-being, I demonstrate my trust in God to provide for my needs as well.

10. I will save a portion of all my earnings knowing that I must always be prepared for unexpected needs and have resources available to serve others.

11. By God's grace, I pledge to never compromise my integrity, despite any short-term cost.

12. Regardless of how much or little I have, I will seek to use all available resources for God's purposes during the time I have on earth. I will make generosity the focus of my life knowing that is the highest privilege to give or share with others all that God has given me.

Signed _____

Date _____

ACKNOWLEDGMENTS

Neither a life nor a book is ever the work of a single person. We are all a product of the input of those who have shaped our lives. I have so many to whom I am eternally grateful. Since this is my first book, I want to express my gratitude to those who have directly impacted my view of true riches and made this work a reality.

Ann Wagner Bentley

Without your love for God, His Word and persistent prayers for me, I may never have experienced the true riches of Christ. Thank you for supporting our family, our mission and me with all of your heart and soul and for your invaluable insights to make this book possible. May you share in the joy of all that God may do in the lives of those who read this book. I love you.

Hank, Lindsay and Henry Bentley,
Todd Bentley, John Bentley, Luke Bentley

Each of you paid the price for the countless hours I have sat with my laptop in front of my face, blocking out all the world around me to press a single key to make the words, sentences and phrases in this manuscript. Just when we thought it was over, I reviewed it, reworked it and reviewed it some more. For your understanding, sacrifice, and support, I am deeply grateful. Each one of you is the real evidence of God's promise that we would *"be made rich in every way."* Thank you for bringing such joy into our lives. You are loved beyond measure.

Jim Henry and Jim Armstrong

You have provided the editorial expertise, insights, layout, design and shaping to make my original manuscript a real book.

I handed you a bowl of spaghetti and you gave it back in a cohesive, organized document worthy of publication. You are godly men, true professionals, great friends and a joy to work with.

Megan Pacheco

You took hold of the project, set up timelines and processes to bring all the pieces together. You inspired me, organized the team and saw it through to completion. Your remarkable gifts, insights and genuine enthusiasm to serve God's people make you a world-class asset to the body of Christ.

Lee Holcomb

Thank you for believing in the project and putting your talents behind the effort.

Christopher Tobias, Kevin Campbell, Kevin Light, Lewis Moats, Sean Allen, Josh Merriam

Each added your creative talents to bring the message to life through visual communication. What started with an idea about a root became a complete book because each of your artistic gifts. Thank you for allowing God to bring this important analogy of our lives compared to trees into a reality for others to share. You contributions are priceless.

Raymond Harris

Thank you for inspiring me to dig deep on this issue of the heart. On countless occasions you have helped bear my burdens, motivated me to press on, and taught me to go "all in" for the Lord's purposes. You have demonstrated the essence of a He Tree to me.

Jack Alexander

You are a constant encourager and mentor. When you like something I have shared, I view it as a strong validation, so I pursue it with vigor, knowing you always speak the truth. The day you heard me teach on this topic and said, "I think every Christian in the world should hear this," I decided it was worthy of the effort to write. Those words have motivated me to finish the task you hold in your hands.

Charles and Sandy Raymond

You have known about the root of riches far longer than me. Your example, passion for God's kingdom and friendship are precious treasures to me.

Chris and Kathy Vochoska

You lead the Crown small group study that God used to radically change my life. I consider myself fruit of your ministry. Thank you for demonstrating what He Trees really look like.

Colleagues

Dave Ball, Bob Dickie, Sheila Thompson, Johnny Franklin, Joe Coney, Tracey Fries, Susan Ellington, Dave Scobey, Jan and Alet Strydom, Peter Briscoe, Ngee Khoon Hoong, Cora Chan, Donald Wu, Paul Shin, Dr. Suparno Adijanto, Wilson Cheah, Rod Rattray, Jorge and Marcia Nishimura and Dr. Frank Gonzalez.

At Crown Financial Ministries, I have the privilege of working with genuine He Trees who are committed to a common vision. You are each great colleagues and multipliers of one of God's most important and relevant movements in the world today.

Brothers in Christ

Stan Reiff, Morgan Jackson, Randy Alcorn, Dean Jones, Hugh O. Maclellan, Ron Blue, Vince Burley, Patrick Johnson, Lee Riffe, Rob Moll, Tyler Burke, Wayne Smith, Daryl Heald, Paul Bagnoli, Steve Magdelin, Jim Shoemaker, Marlin Horst,

Andre Styger, James Thweatt, Jack Young, Tom Darden, Dr. Peter Zhao, Phil Clemens, Steve Douglass, Jim Daly, Ken Hamm, Jim Green, Bill Williams, Loren Cunningham, David Hamilton, Eddie Staub, Gage Prichard, Phil Drake, John Piper, John Batusik, Reginaldo Kruklis, Kennedy Smart, David Wills, Rusty Leonard, Dale Brooks, Gunnar Johnson, Jason Cunningham, Jason Garcia, Paulo Maximiano, Nobu Handa, Dinart Barradas, Benji Song, Greg Fast, Handre de Jongh, Dr. Jong Park, Dr. Y.K. Wenn, Cannon James Wong, Eric Lai, Matt Ellsberry, Jon Spear, Peter Greer, Jim Sullivan, Steve Brooks, John Riley, Jeff Anderson, Steve Whaley, Chris Steiger, Dr. Jim Froelich, Chuck Swindoll, Andy Blakeslee, John Parker, Tommy Beck, Scott Melby, Kurt Buehlmann, Hal White, David Heinrich, Jon and Andy Erwin and my "real" brother, John Bentley.

I am especially grateful to you whose interlocking roots have helped me at key times in my walk with Christ.

Larry Burkett and Howard Dayton

Thank you for your life work that has served to multiply He Trees around the world. I consider myself as one among the millions that your lives have touched and remain eternally grateful for what I have learned from each of you.

Mom & Dad, Karen & Don, Phyllis & Roy, Rocky & Cindy, John & Mere

I love you and am grateful to be in a family that loves the Lord.

HOW TO KNOW OUR TREE OF LIFE

As important as our financial welfare is, it is not our highest priority. The single most important need of every person everywhere is to know God and experience the gift of His forgiveness and peace.

These five biblical truths will show you God's open door through a personal relationship with Jesus Christ.

1. God loves you and wants you to know Him and experience a meaningful life.

God created people in His own image, and He desires a close relationship with each of us. *"For God so loved the world, that He gave His only begotten Son, that whoever believes in Him shall not perish, but have eternal life"* (John 3:16). *"I [Jesus] came that they might have life, and have it abundantly"* (John 10:10).

God the Father loved you so much that He gave His only Son, Jesus Christ, to die for you.

2. Unfortunately, we are separated from God.

Because God is holy and perfect, no sin can abide in His presence. Every person has sinned, and the consequence of sin is separation from God. *"All have sinned and fall short of the glory of God"* (Romans 3:23). *"Your sins have cut you off from God"* (Isaiah 59:2, TLB).

3.   God's only provision to bridge this gap is Jesus Christ.

Jesus Christ died on the cross to pay the penalty for our sin, bridging the gap between God and us. Jesus said, *"I am the way, and the truth, and the life; no one comes to the Father but through Me"* (John 14:6). *"God demonstrates His own love towards us, in that while we were yet sinners, Christ died for us"* (Romans 5:8).

4.   This relationship is a gift from God.

Our efforts can never achieve the perfection God requires. The only solution was to provide it for us as a gift.

When Jesus bore our sins on the cross, paying our penalty forever, He exchanged His righteousness for our guilt. By faith, we receive the gift we could never deserve.

"It is by grace you have been saved, through faith—and this is not from yourselves, it is the gift of God—not by works, so that no one can boast" (Ephesians 2:8-9, NIV).

5.   We must each receive Jesus Christ individually.

Someone has said that God has no grandchildren. Each of us is responsible before God for our own sin. We can continue to bear the responsibility and pay the consequences or we can receive the gift of Jesus' righteousness, enabling God to declare us "Not guilty!"

If you desire to know the Lord and are not certain whether you have this relationship, we encourage you to ask Christ into your heart right now. Pray a prayer similar to this suggested one:

"God, I need You. I invite Jesus to come into my life as my Savior and Lord and to make me the person You want me to be. Thank You for forgiving my sins and for giving me the gift of eternal life."

You may be successful in avoiding financial quicksand—and we pray you will be—but without a relationship with Christ, it won't have lasting value. Eternal perspective begins with Him.

If you ask Christ into your life, please tell some people you know who are also following Christ. They will encourage you and help you get involved in a Bible-teaching church where you can grow spiritually. And please let us know as well. We would love to help in any way we can.

ABOUT CROWN FINANCIAL MINISTRIES

Crown's vision is to see the followers of Christ in every nation faithfully living by God's financial principles in every area of their life so they are free to serve Him more fully. As an interdenominational Christian ministry, Crown serves people seeking to improve their personal finances, businesses and careers.

Crown employs a variety of media, including dramatic films, video, radio, podcasts, seminars and small group studies to achieve this end. Our mission is accomplished through a global network of dedicated staff and volunteers.

Founded in 1976, Crown Financial Ministries is a 501(c)(3) nonprofit educational organization. Headquartered in the suburbs of Atlanta, Georgia, Crown has operations in cities across the United States and is active on five continents.

We invite you to get acquainted with us. It is our privilege to serve you.

Crown.org

ABOUT CHUCK BENTLEY

For over a decade, Chuck Bentley has traveled the world teaching biblical financial principles to the affluent, middle class, poor and ultra poor. As host of the daily national radio broadcast, *My MoneyLife*™, Chuck connects with all generations and inspires his audience with a strong scriptural emphasis.

Following in the footsteps of Crown's cofounders, Howard Dayton and the late Larry Burkett, Chuck leads Crown Financial Ministries, an organization founded in the Atlanta area in 1976 that now reaches around the world with staff or volunteers on every continent.

Chuck is the executive producer of the *God Provides*™ *Film Learning Experience*, Crown's first series of short films. He is also the co-creator of the *Crown Money Map*™ and a contributor to Saddleback Church's small group series, *Managing Our Finances God's Way*. These powerful resources are being used to transform lives around the world.

A Texas native, Chuck is a graduate of Baylor University, where he earned a bachelor's degree in Business Administration. He is a frequent speaker on biblical financial topics at church and business functions.

Chuck and his wife, Ann, were married in 1978. They live near Atlanta, Georgia and have four sons, a daughter-in-law, and a grandson. Chuck enjoys reading, the outdoors and spending time with his family.

You can stay in touch with Chuck, follow his blog, join Facebook and Twitter and be a part of the global community who share *The Root of Riches*—all at Crown.org.

GROUP STUDY

W e strongly encourage you to use *The Root of Riches* as the basis for a truly life-changing group study. You can begin to transform the nation and the world with your small group. Here's all you need to know to get started today:

- As a facilitator, you don't need to be an expert, just familiar with the content of the book. Before the study begins, simply review and answer the questions at the end of each chapter.

- The format and how much content to cover is entirely up to you as the facilitator. Just remember to leave time for everyone to participate and to ask questions.

- To encourage trust and open communication, assure everyone that what is said in the group stays in the group.

- Speak less and encourage others to speak more. Avoid monologues. Engage participants through insightful questions, and listen carefully to every response.

- If someone asks a question that you can't answer, say so and offer to track down the answer later or guide the person to someone else who knows it.

- It's vitally important to learn new truths and evaluate how they relate to daily life. As the facilitator, share how you are applying, or plan to apply, truths you are learning.

- Use the questions provided, but don't feel you need to cover all of them. Never cut off meaningful discussion.

- Few people are Bible scholars, and participants will be at various stages in their financial and spiritual journeys. Read aloud the recommended verses at the end of each chapter to guide discussion toward biblical answers without criticism or judgment.

- This is serious business, but don't be afraid to use a little humor whenever possible to lighten the atmosphere.

Crown has a variety of practical learning options—group studies, one-on-one budget coaching, live seminars, and more. Let us come alongside as you take the next step in building a holistic teaching ministry that focuses on the stewardship of time, talent and treasure. Please contact us at 1-800-722-1976 or visit us online at Crown.org.